Editor
Eric Migliaccio

Editor in Chief
Karen J. Goldfluss, M.S. Ed.

Cover Artist
Barb Lorseyedi

Illustrator
Clint McKnight

Art Coordinator
Renée Mc Elwee

Imaging
James Edward Grace

Publisher

Mary D. Smith, M.S. Ed.

Author
Heather Wolpert-Gawron

For information about Common Core State Standards, see pages 4–6 of this book or visit *http://www.teachercreated.com/standards*

Teacher Created Resources
6421 Industry Way
Westminster, CA 92683
www.teachercreated.com
ISBN: 978-1-4206-2789-3
© 2014 Teacher Created Resources
Made in U.S.A.

Table of Contents

Common Core State Standards 4

Introduction: Nothing Fits in a Box Anymore 7

How To Use This Book 8

I. Project-Based Writing and the Multi-Genre Approach 10

What Is Project-Based Writing? — 10 Reasons to Teach Project-Based Writing — The Multi-Genre Approach — Differentiation in Education

II. Creating a Project-Based Writing Unit 14

Choosing a Topic or Theme — The Student-Created Resource Library — What Are the Parts of a Unit? — A List of Multi-Genre Elements — Using a Unit Checklist — What Will a Completed Project Look Like?

III. Resources

A. Activities
Playing Think–Tac–Toe 20

Getting a Reader's Attention. 21

Comparing Skills: Quoting vs. Paraphrasing 22

Revealing a Theme. 24

"Finding" a Poem 26

Creating Literary Hybrids 27

Mastering the Art of the Article 28

Conducting a Movement Survey 30

Learning from the Experts 33

Creating a Homepage 34

Using Technology to Present. 35

Writing a Recipe for "Success" 36

Reading and Writing a Script 38

Mimicking an Artist's Style. 39

Using an Illuminated Letter 40

Using an Illuminated Border. 41

Creating a Comic Strip 42

Making a Flip Book. 44

Wrapping It All Up 45

Table of Contents *(cont.)*

III. Resources *(cont.)*

B. Research

Cornell Notes 46

Bibliographies 48

C. Organization

Outline — Narrative/Story 50

Outline — Persuasive 52

Outline — Summary 53

Outline — Response to Literature 54

The Writing-Genre Matrix 55

Unit Checklist 56

D. Assessment

Using Rubrics 57

> Teacher-Created Rubrics — Student-Created Rubrics

Teacher Feedback 60

IV. Pre-Made Project-Based Writing Units

Unit 1: Teach the Teacher 61

> Teachable Topics — How Learners Learn — Pitch Your Topic — Create a Lesson Plan — Quiz the Class — Give an Oral Presentation — Write a Persuasive Letter — Unit Checklist

Unit 2: Career Quest Project 75

> Research a Future Career — Write a Resume — Develop a Cover Letter — Answer a Help-Wanted Ad — The Job Interview — Unit Checklist

Unit 3: Advocacy Research Project 87

> Zeroing In on a Topic — Write a Thesis Statement — Conduct an Interview — Create a Graph — Unit Checklist

Common Core State Standards

Project-Based Writing, Grades 6–8 gives students and teachers the necessary resources and ideas needed to create project-based-writing units in the classroom. During each step of this process, students will engage in activities that meet one or more of the following Common Core State Standards. (©Copyright 2010. National Governors Association Center for Best Practices and Council of Chief State School Officers. All rights reserved.) For more information about the Common Core State Standards, go to *http://www.corestandards.org/* or *http://teachercreated.com/standards/*.

	Informational Text Standards
Key Ideas and Details	
ELA.RI.6.1	Cite textual evidence to support analysis of what the text says explicitly as well as inferences drawn from the text.
ELA.RI.7.1	Cite several pieces of textual evidence to support analysis of what the text says explicitly as well as inferences drawn from the text.
ELA.RI.8.1	Cite the textual evidence that most strongly supports an analysis of what the text says explicitly as well as inferences drawn from the text.
ELA.RI.6.2	Determine a central idea of a text and how it is conveyed through particular details; provide a summary of the text distinct from personal opinions or judgments.
ELA.RI.7.2	Determine two or more central ideas in a text and analyze their development over the course of the text; provide an objective summary of the text.
ELA.RI.8.2	Determine a central idea of a text and analyze its development over the course of the text, including its relationship to supporting ideas; provide an objective summary of the text.
Craft and Structure	
ELA.RI.6.4	Determine the meaning of words and phrases as they are used in a text, including figurative, connotative, and technical meanings.
ELA.RI.7.4	Determine the meaning of words and phrases as they are used in a text, including figurative, connotative, and technical meanings; analyze the impact of a specific word choice on meaning and tone.
ELA.RI.8.4	Determine the meaning of words and phrases as they are used in a text, including figurative, connotative, and technical meanings; analyze the impact of specific word choices on meaning and tone, including analogies or allusions to other texts.
ELA.RI.6.5	Analyze how a particular sentence, paragraph, chapter, or section fits into the overall structure of a text and contributes to the development of the ideas.
ELA.RI.7.5	Analyze the structure an author uses to organize a text, including how the major sections contribute to the whole and to the development of the ideas.
ELA.RI.8.5	Analyze in detail the structure of a specific paragraph in a text, including the role of particular sentences in developing and refining a key concept.
Integration of Knowledge and Ideas	
ELA.RI.6.7	Integrate information presented in different media or formats (e.g., visually, quantitatively) as well as in words to develop a coherent understanding of a topic or issue.
ELA.RI.7.7	Compare and contrast a text to an audio, video, or multimedia version of the text, analyzing each medium's portrayal of the subject (e.g., how the delivery of a speech affects the impact of the words).
ELA.RI.8.7	Evaluate the advantages and disadvantages of using different mediums (e.g., print or digital text, video, multimedia) to present a particular topic or idea.

Common Core State Standards *(cont.)*

Informational Text Standards *(cont.)*	
Integration of Knowledge and Ideas *(cont.)*	
ELA.RI.6.8	Trace and evaluate the argument and specific claims in a text, distinguishing claims that are supported by reasons and evidence from claims that are not.
ELA.RI.7.8	Trace and evaluate the argument and specific claims in a text, assessing whether the reasoning is sound and the evidence is relevant and sufficient to support the claims.
ELA.RI.8.8	Delineate and evaluate the argument and specific claims in a text, assessing whether the reasoning is sound and the evidence is relevant and sufficient; recognize when irrelevant evidence is introduced.
Range of Reading and Level of Text Complexity	
ELA.RI.6.10 **ELA.RI.7.10**	By the end of the year, read and comprehend literary nonfiction in the grades 6–8 text complexity band proficiently, with scaffolding as needed at the high end of the range.
ELA.RI.8.10	By the end of the year, read and comprehend literary nonfiction at the high end of the grades 6–8 text complexity band independently and proficiently.
Writing Standards	
Text Types and Purposes	
ELA.W.6.1 **ELA.W.7.1** **ELA.W.8.1**	Write arguments to support claims with clear reasons and relevant evidence.
ELA.W.6.2 **ELA.W.7.2** **ELA.W.8.2**	Write informative/explanatory texts to examine a topic and convey ideas, concepts, and information through the selection, organization, and analysis of relevant content.
ELA.W.6.3 **ELA.W.7.3** **ELA.W.8.3**	Write narratives to develop real or imagined experiences or events using effective technique, relevant descriptive details, and well-structured event sequences.
Production and Distribution of Writing	
ELA.W.6.4 **ELA.W.7.4** **ELA.W.8.4**	Produce clear and coherent writing in which the development, organization, and style are appropriate to task, purpose, and audience.
ELA.W.6.5	With some guidance and support from peers and adults, develop and strengthen writing as needed by planning, revising, editing, rewriting, or trying a new approach.
ELA.W.7.5 **ELA.W.8.5**	With some guidance and support from peers and adults, develop and strengthen writing as needed by planning, revising, editing, rewriting, or trying a new approach, focusing on how well purpose and audience have been addressed.
ELA.W.6.6	Use technology, including the Internet, to produce and publish writing as well as to interact and collaborate with others; demonstrate sufficient command of keyboarding skills to type a minimum of three pages in a single sitting.
ELA.W.7.6	Use technology, including the Internet, to produce and publish writing and link to and cite sources as well as to interact and collaborate with others, including linking to and citing sources.

Common Core State Standards *(cont.)*

Writing Standards *(cont.)*	
Production and Distribution of Writing *(cont.)*	
ELA.W.8.6	Use technology, including the Internet, to produce and publish writing and present the relationships between information and ideas efficiently as well as to interact and collaborate with others.
Research to Build and Present Knowledge	
ELA.W.6.7	Conduct short research projects to answer a question, drawing on several sources and refocusing the inquiry when appropriate.
ELA.W.7.7	Conduct short research projects to answer a question, drawing on several sources and generating additional related, focused questions for further research and investigation.
ELA.W.8.7	Conduct short research projects to answer a question (including a self-generated question), drawing on several sources and generating additional related, focused questions that allow for multiple avenues of exploration.
ELA.W.6.8	Gather relevant information from multiple print and digital sources; assess the credibility of each source; and quote or paraphrase the data and conclusions of others while avoiding plagiarism and providing basic bibliographic information for sources.
ELA.W.7.8 **ELA.W.8.8**	Gather relevant information from multiple print and digital sources, using search terms effectively; assess the credibility and accuracy of each source; and quote or paraphrase the data and conclusions of others while avoiding plagiarism
ELA.W.6.9 **ELA.W.7.9** **ELA.W.8.9**	Draw evidence from literary or informational texts to support analysis, reflection, and research.
Speaking and Listening Standards	
Comprehension and Collaboration	
ELA.SL.6.1 **ELA.SL.7.1** **ELA.SL.8.1**	Engage effectively in a range of collaborative discussions (one-on-one, in groups, and teacher-led) with diverse partners on grade-level topics, texts, and issues, building on others' ideas and expressing their own clearly.
Presentation of Knowledge and Ideas	
ELA.SL.6.4	Present claims and findings, sequencing ideas logically and using pertinent descriptions, facts, and details to accentuate main ideas or themes; use appropriate eye contact, adequate volume, and clear pronunciation.
ELA.SL.7.4	Present claims and findings, emphasizing salient points in a focused, coherent manner with pertinent descriptions, facts, details, and examples; use appropriate eye contact, adequate volume, and clear pronunciation.
ELA.SL.8.4	Present claims and findings, emphasizing salient points in a focused, coherent manner with relevant evidence, sound valid reasoning, and well-chosen details; use appropriate eye contact, adequate volume, and clear pronunciation.
ELA.SL.6.5	Include multimedia components (e.g., graphics, images, music, sound) and visual displays in presentations to clarify information.
ELA.SL.7.5	Include multimedia components and visual displays in presentations to clarify claims and findings and emphasize salient points.
ELA.SL.8.5	Integrate multimedia and visual displays into presentations to clarify information, strengthen claims and evidence, and add interest.

Introduction:
Nothing Fits in a Box Anymore

This book and the concepts contained within it are a direct response to the growing trend toward differentiation and individualization. The multi-genre, hybrid approach of *Project-Based Writing* recognizes the differences between students, how they learn, and how they seek to show their learning. It caters to their individual strengths, while also guiding them toward the exploration of other means of expression that they might instinctively tend to avoid.

Ultimately, project-based writing is about choice. Just as we live in a culture in which every person in the coffee line can have his or her own personalized beverage made to order, so, too, should students be given the tools and the opportunity to show off their knowledge in many different ways.

A vital aspect of project-based writing is the blending of school life with real life. Often, there is a disconnect between the two. Many students, especially tweens and teens, see school life as totally separate from life outside of school. Therefore, it becomes our job as teachers to make sure that the classroom more directly correlates to the outside world. Choice is a huge part of doing that. So whenever possible in your curriculum, you should feel encouraged to offer student choice, while of course still emphasizing academic rigor and content knowledge.

The multi-genre activities and units covered in *Project-Based Writing* offer the best of both worlds: students gain a functional knowledge of a whole slew of genres, formats, and ways of expressing themselves; and at the same time, they learn to successfully weave these separate elements together into a cohesive whole that digs deeper into the topics, themes, and issues that are most important to their lives outside of school. It is this step of integration that moves students beyond the simple regurgitation of ideas and into a higher level of thinking: that of creation.

How To Use This Book

This book is divided into four parts, each designed to help you, the teacher, guide your students in the creation of project-based writing units.

I. Project-Based Writing and the Multi-Genre Approach (pages 10–13)

Here is where you can find an overview of the ideas behind project-based writing and why the multi-genre approach is so vital to engaging your students and enriching their writing.

II. Creating a Project-Based Writing Unit (pages 14–19)

This section shows you how to begin the process of introducing your students to multi-genre projects. This is where you and your students can start to hone in on the topics and themes that most interest them. It's also where you will learn about the elements that make up each project-based writing unit and where you'll get a glimpse at what a finished product could look like.

III. Resources (pages 20–60)

The resources contained within this section are divided into four main categories:

Activities   **Research**   **Organization**   **Assessment**

Collectively — or in any combination you choose — these resources are intended to provide your students with the tools needed to produce projects that are effective, engaging, and unique. Each page is written to the students, and each is designed to serve as a resource your students can refer back to as they work through the creative process. Each new resource in this section begins with a brief statement explaining how it can be helpful in the creation of a project-based writing unit.

A. Activities

Here you'll find the nuts and bolts of any project-based writing unit. These activities are varied and flexible; they span several genres and skills, and they can be introduced in any order. The aim here is to equip your students with an abundance of options and ideas.

B. Research

This section gives your students practical methods for conducting and recording the research they will need to do in order to dig deeper into their topics.

How To Use This Book *(cont.)*

III. Resources *(cont.)*

C. Organization

Students need to pre-plan and structure their work so that they stay focused and on task. The checklists and multiple outlines provided here will help do just that.

D. Assessment

Need a rubric? There are options for different rubrics in this section, as well as a guide to help your students design their own rubrics. Also included is a form that students can use to record your feedback in their own words.

IV. Pre-Made Project-Based Writing Units (pages 61–96)

Finally, this book includes three pre-made project-based writing units that you can use as is, from beginning to end.

For grades 6–8, the three pre-made units are as follows:

Teach the Teacher

Career Quest Project

Advocacy Research Project

Each unit begins with an overview page that provides step-by-step instructions on how to proceed through the unit. You can also dip into the "Activities" section to add or swap out any lesson you wish. It is this ability to interchange lessons and create different combinations of units that makes this concept of project-based writing with a multi-genre emphasis so unique.

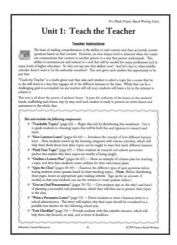

What Is Project-Based Writing?

Project-based writing puts a spin on the concept of project-based learning, which is the act of learning through identifying a real-world problem and developing its solution. The project that results from this endeavor encourages students to use critical-thinking skills to journey towards an authentic goal.

Project-based writing activities strive to meet certain criteria. By design, these activities are . . .

❖ multi-genre.

❖ differentiated.

❖ thematic.

❖ both linguistic and non-linguistic.

❖ cross-curricular.

❖ based on real-world scenarios.

❖ guided by student choice.

❖ filled with 21st-century connections.

Project-based writing argues that any subject — be it language arts or STEM — can benefit from strong writing practice. Any genre of writing can support the other. And any engaging activity that links academic learning to the real world can be a 21st-century tool.

---

10 Reasons to Teach Project-Based Writing

1. It is an organic way to integrate all core subjects — math, science, history, and language arts.

2. It proves to students that imagination and creativity are connected to research and expository writing.

3. It hits all the major elements of the higher levels of Bloom's Taxonomy: Analysis, Evaluation, and Creation.

4. By allowing students to choose their format of showing what they know, the buy-in for the quality of the final project is tremendous.

5. Students develop projects that are individualized, unique, and specific from each other.

6. It is a powerful way to incorporate all multiple intelligences: visual, verbal, logical, musical, physical, social, solitary, and naturalistic.

7. It desegregates nonfiction and fiction, blending the two.

8. It integrates the core subjects with non-core subjects, potentially using technology, art, music, etc.

9. It is a rigorous assessment requiring high levels of thought and communication.

10. It requires use of the entire writing process — from brainstorming to revising, editing, and completing the final draft — regardless of the genres picked and the topic chosen.

The Multi-Genre Approach

At the heart of project-based writing is the concept of melding multiple genres into a final product. This multi-genre approach involves taking several distinct types of writing and fusing them into something unique and powerful. Essentially, a hybrid is created.

Throughout history, humans have strived to create hybrids. In science, people have bred their ideal loyal companion in the Golden Retriever or created their perfect salad accessory in the bug-resistant tomato. In literature, authors and storytellers have written about hybrids, such as the unicorn and Pegasus.

Here are some examples of hybrids throughout history:

Picture	Description
	half electric, half gasoline-powered
	half person, half fish
	half Labrador, half poodle
	half chocolate, half peanut butter

In project-based writing, a hybrid is created when we combine genres that revolve around a shared topic or theme. The result is a multi-genre project that uses the best of different presentations and weaves them together into a totally new creature.

After all, just as any subject can benefit from strong writing practice, so can any genre of writing help support another. The multi-genre aspect of project-based writing is important because it is vital that students understand that genres are not compartmentalized in life. For example, a narrative can support a persuasive argument, just as a graph can support a summary. Weaving the strengths of multiple genres together into one project is the key to project-based writing and to providing one's audience with a richer, fuller picture of a topic or theme.

Differentiation in Education

As you know, there are many different kinds of learners out there in the classrooms. Some students like to write, others like to sing; some like to play sports, while others like to draw. A multi-genre approach allows students to choose ways to show off what they know and what they've learned about a topic, using the methods that are the most interesting to them. Just as importantly, it allows them to challenge themselves and present topics using methods that are not normally in their nature to attempt. So by requiring students to display their content knowledge in multiple ways, you are allowing them to operate within their comfort zones on the one hand, while also pushing them to more fully develop a technique that is challenging to them.

21st-Century Connection: Many students know what interests them, what kind of learner they are, and how they most like to display their knowledge. But it's also very empowering for them to take quizzes that help them identify their natural instincts. With that in mind, consider having students take a test to identify the style in which they learn best. One such four-part quiz is available at The George Lucas Foundation's website, Edutopia.org:

http://www.edutopia.org/multiple-intelligences-learning-styles-quiz

PAGE 1 OF 4

How much time do you spend:

	NONE	ONLY A LITTLE	A FAIR AMOUNT	A LOT	ALL THE TIME
Getting lost in a good book.	○	○	○	○	○
Doing crafts or arts projects.	○	○	○	○	○
Trying to solve mysteries, riddles, or crossword puzzles.	○	○	○	○	○
Writing a journal or blogging.	○	○	○	○	○
Reflecting on your life and your future.	○	○	○	○	○
Playing sports.	○	○	○	○	○
Yearning to spend time with nature.	○	○	○	○	○

(Next Page >)

See page 13 for a complete breakdown of the different types of learners that you may have in your classroom.

Differentiation in Education *(cont.)*

Because we hear so much about differentiation in education, let's take a moment to look more closely at the different ways people learn—and just as importantly for purposes of project-based writing, the different ways people best show what they've learned. This information is usually referred to as "multiple intelligences." Consult the following chart:

The Multiple Intelligences	Some Ways They Learn/Show What They Know
Visual/Spatial	puzzles, maps, 3-D models, charts, graphs, architecture
Verbal/Linguistic	reading, word games, poetry, speeches, lectures
Logical/Mathematical	patterns, puzzles, experiments, investigations, mysteries
Musical/Auditory	songs, lyrics, rhythmic speaking, dance, musical instruments
Physical/Kinesthetic	movement, hands-on activities, acting out, role-playing, realia
Social/Interpersonal	interaction, dialogue, group dynamics, e-mail, video conferencing
Solitary/Intrapersonal	introspection, diaries, journals, books, independent study
Naturalistic	walks; digging; collecting; using microscopes, telescopes, maps, and globes

Choosing a Topic or Theme

The first step a student must take in creating a project-based writing unit is choosing a topic that piques his or her interest. When thinking about a topic, the student might want to choose one with which he or she is somewhat familiar but could learn more about through research. On the other hand, the student could choose a topic he or she has always wanted to know more about but hasn't had the opportunity to explore in detail.

An ideal topic could be anything from a historical event or person to a hot-topic issue that the student wishes to advocate for or argue against.

A theme-based project is another option to consider. Themes, however, can often be discovered and uncovered midway through a topic-based project. (For an activity page on revealing themes, see pages 24–25 in the "Resources" section.)

Where to Find Topics

Topics are always out there, ready to be dissected and discussed. Here are just a few of the many possibilities you can present to your students:

❖ **Historical Events or People** — The Black Death • Battle of Gettysburg • Declaration of Independence • Underground Railroad • Emancipation Proclamation • The Crusades • Trojan War • Eruption of Mt. Vesuvius • Abraham Lincoln • Ferdinand Magellan • Henry VIII • Julius Caesar • Hatshepsut • Queen Elizabeth • Lorenzo de' Medici • Sacagawea

❖ **Writers/Artists/Scientists** — Leonardo da Vinci • Michelangelo • Donatello • William Shakespeare • Galileo • Copernicus • Lamarck • Kepler

❖ **Recent Events or People** — September 11, 2001 • The Dot-Com Bubble • The Housing Boom and Crash • Bill Gates • Barack Obama • Lance Armstrong • Muhammad Ali • Danica Patrick • Hurricane Katrina • Japan Earthquake and Tsunami of 2011

❖ **Advocacy Issues** — Single-Sex Schools • Paying Students for Grades • Paying Students for Attendance • Global Warming • School Budgets • Cloning • Dress Code • Gum Chewing • Cell-Phone Usage • Autism • Eating Disorders

❖ **Themes** — Change • Courage • Acceptance • Loyalty • Success • Aging • Overcoming Adversity

❖ **Morals** — "Beauty is only skin deep." • "Birds of a feather flock together." • "Live and let live." • "Look before you leap."

You may choose to present these to your class, or you could opt for topics that align more closely with your class's curriculum. A list of possible topics could serve as a way to jumpstart your students' thought processes about what kinds of subjects would provide the basis for dynamic project-based writing units.

The Student-Created Resource Library

It's true that you can use the traditional way of having students find their sources, research their topics, and collect their data. But instead, consider making research a collaborative, community-building project for the entire classroom.

Imagine an area of the classroom filled with the resources brought in by the students. As students discover reference material, articles, and chapters from outside the classroom, they bring copies of the material into the classroom and file them in this location for other students to use.

It's easy to start. First, assign a typical advocacy topic that can be found in many different formats. Take, for example, the topic of global warming. Okay, so you've asked students to bring in copies of articles, book pages, etc., all on global warming. Create a file called "Global Warming" and place it in a special file box called "Resource Library." File all of the resources into it.

Try it as a weekly current-events assignment leading up to a research report. It's possible that by the time the students have to actually select a topic, you will have a resource library already under way for that topic.

The great part of this is that it's a growing, dynamic library. As kids settle on their topics, they continue to research and add to the files.

In addition, to encourage further collaboration, keep a chart in the classroom with everyone's names and selected topics so that when students come across research that relates to a peer's topic, they can refer that student to the evidence they found. It's a collaborative form of research that uses the classroom as a working, growing reference library.

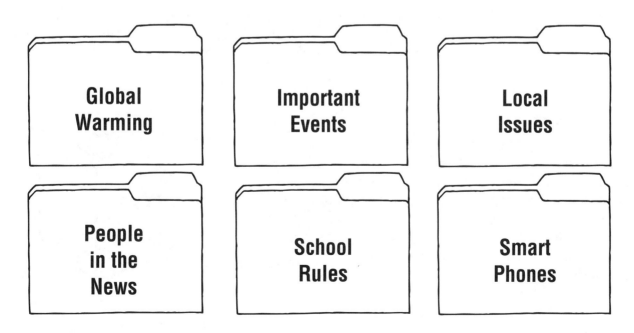

What Are the Parts of a Unit?

In order to create a project-based writing unit, students will use many skills and work in multiple genres. They will do this in all of the steps of the creation process, from planning and research to writing and the production of a final project. This final product will consist of two basic parts: the multi-genre elements and the container.

> *See page 19 for examples of containers and the multi-genre elements they could contain.*

The Multi-Genre Elements

Once students choose the topic or theme on which they will build their projects, they next should begin to think about what elements will make up their final project. These multi-genre elements will comprise the bulk of the project, and they will ideally be a mixture of multiple written and visual genres. In order to really challenge themselves (and also explore more nuances of their topics and themes), students should work not just with the elements with which they are most comfortable. While a visual learner is encouraged to use all of the elements that align with his or her instinctual abilities (say, creating comic books and designing website homepages), that student is also expected to consider penning a persuasive essay or crafting a campaign speech that further illuminates the topic.

A list of possible multi-genre elements is included on the following page. While there is some overlap, the elements are divided into columns depending on whether they are primarily written or visual. You may wish to copy this list and distribute one to each student. Have your students examine each column and circle those activities that they may find interesting to create and that will best illustrate their chosen issue or topic. Also, allow students to add new ideas to the list. As long as the element enriches their project, students should be encouraged to let their imaginations soar.

> *Many of these elements are explored individually and in greater detail on pages 20–45 of the "Activities" section.*

The Container

One important guiding principle for students to keep in mind is that a project's final appearance will function best if it reflects the theme or subject that it is based on. An appropriate container will go a long way in accomplishing this. Whether it is simple or elaborate, it should function as the final piece that ties all of the other pieces together. Think of the container as the visual delivery system for the project.

A List of Multi-Genre Elements

Directions: Below are lists of possible elements you can combine for use in a project. Examine each column and circle the ones that you may find interesting to create and that will best illustrate your chosen issue or topic. If any other ideas occur to you, record them in the spaces at the bottom of the appropriate column.

Written (Linguistic)	Visual (Non-Linguistic)	Other
Campaign Speech	Advertisement	Directions
Character Sketch	Family Tree	Recipe
Dialogue	Greeting Card	Quiz
Essay	Website	How-to Guide
Fable or Fairy Tale	Picture Book	List
Website	Map	Song
Poetry	Postcard	Dance
Diary Entry	Movie Poster	Board Game
Blog	Diorama	Computer Game
Memoir	Flip Book	Reader's Theater
News Article	Building-Blocks Structure	Podcast
Op-ed Piece	Statue	Video
Petition	Comic Book	Monologue
Advocacy Essay	Comic Life (using iLife suite)	
Letters	Prezi	
Review	PowerPoint	
Script	Blueprint (using Google Sketch-up)	
Glossary		
Narrative		
Interview		
Legend		
Letter of Complaint		
Summary		

Using a Unit Checklist

A checklist is an effective organizational tool that can help students remember what's due and when. There are many different ways to format a checklist. The three pre-made units in this workbook (pages 61–96), for example, contain checklists that are tailored to those projects.

The sample checklist below can give you an idea of appropriate expectations you could have for each student to include in his or her writing unit. For the project below, you may instruct students that the top three assignments must be included. From there, they could be asked to choose one activity from each of the other categories, ensuring that the completed project contains seven pieces in all. This is just one way to approach assigning a unit's components.

Note: A blank checklist is provided on page 56 in the "Resources" section.

Date Due	Date Completed	Assigned Element	Possibilities
		Persuasive Pitch to Teacher About Topic	❖ Letter ❖ Essay
		Research	❖ Cornell Notes ❖ Quickwrites ❖ Movement Survey
		Bibliography/Works Cited	❖ n/a
		Written Piece	❖ Narrative ❖ Poem ❖ Glossary/Dictionary ❖ Interview/Dialogue ❖ Biography ❖ Diary Entry
		Visual or Technological Element	❖ Poster/Ad ❖ Cartoon ❖ PowerPoint/Prezi ❖ Website ❖ Board Game
		Mathematical Piece	❖ Map ❖ Recipe ❖ Step-by-Step Guide
		Musical or Movement-Based Piece	❖ Cover Song ❖ Original Song ❖ Dance

What Will a Completed Project Look Like?

So what should a completed project-based writing unit look like? The short answer is that there is no one design for how these units should look. In fact, the hope is that each student project looks unique in its display and is specific in its content. Individuality is not only encouraged, it is essential to the concept. Here are two examples:

Project Topic/Theme: Childhood Obesity
Container/Format: Pizza Box

Project Topic/Theme: Pollution
Container/Format: Tri-Board Display

Includes: *a research paper on pollution, a science-fiction narrative about a future in which the world has been taken over by trash, comic-book frames illustrating key moments from the narrative, a recipe of the ingredients that make up a dump site, a student-created quiz, the answers to which can be found in the contents of the project*

Playing Think–Tac–Toe

Project-Based Writing Connection: Use this resource as a brainstorming activity or to help you begin rough drafts for your projects.

Get your creative juices flowing by using these prompts to write about your topic.

Directions: Pick three prompts in a row — either across or diagonally — and follow the directions. Use a separate piece of paper for your responses.

	Narrative	**Response to Literature**	**Persuasive**
Row 1	Write a story in which the main character completely changes his or her mind about something important by the end of the story.	Find an essay, poem, or piece of art connected to your topic and respond to the author's main message.	Take a stance on your topic and create an ad that displays your stance.
Row 2	Write a story that begins in the middle of an action-packed scene related to your topic.	Find a blog, letter, column, or poem connected to your issue. Rewrite it any way you want. Then write a note explaining what you changed and why.	In a one-page essay, take a stance on your topic and persuade the reader to agree with you.
Row 3	Make up a fairy tale about your topic. Include a moral or lesson at the end.	Find a story, poem, or piece of art connected to your topic and write an analysis of the main character's traits.	Write a persuasive letter to your school principal about your topic.

Getting a Reader's Attention

Project-Based Writing Connection: When adding a written component to your project, use a hook to grab your reader's attention right from the start.

A *hook* is that first moment of a paper — be it a narrative or an essay — that catches the reader's attention and makes him or her want to read more.

Below is a list of hooks using different strategies to begin the same essay: a piece written about the plague known as "the Black Death." As you can see, there are many ways to hook a reader.

1. **Fact/Statistic** Nearly 1/3 of the population of Europe was killed by the plague.	2. **Tone/Mood** The bodies piled up in the streets of London, untouched, uncared for, mourned by the frightened masses who were left wondering when it would be their turn to die.
3. **Simile/Metaphor** The Black Death swept across the land like a broom brushing away people as if they were dirt.	4. **In the Middle of the Action** The trebuchet cranked back slowly, then released suddenly, launching the body up and over the walls of the city.
5. **Definition** The Black Death was an unstoppable disease caused by the fleas carried by the rats that cohabitated with the people of Medieval Europe.	6. **Onomatopoeia** Sssssss. Sizzle. The fever burned through the victim's body.
7. **Dialogue** "I see there's been no improvement," the apothecary sadly admitted, looking at the small girl before him trembling and sweating with fever.	8. **Staccato Three-Word Lead** Rats. Sewers. Filth. London was not a city of great cleanliness.
9. **Lyrics** "Ring around the rosie. Pockets full of posies. Ashes, ashes, we all fall down!"	10. **Theme** Some people believed that the Plague was sent to punish the evil on Earth, but they would soon learn that the disease knew no such ethics. It did not distinguish its victims.

Directions: After reading each of the examples above, think of an essay you are working on. You may be revising or just beginning. Try to start the piece of writing using each of these strategies. Then, pass your new list of hooks to your peer. Have your classmate circle the three he or she feels are the strongest. Pick one of these three hooks to use when writing or revising.

Comparing Skills:
Quoting vs. Paraphrasing

Project-Based Writing Connection: Paraphrasing and quoting are similar, yet different, tools that can be used to persuade a reader, analyze an argument, or move a story along.

Quoting and *paraphrasing* are two different skills, each with its own purpose.

Think of them this way:

Quoting	**Paraphrasing**
giving an exact, word-for-word piece of text that has been *copied from another source*	*using your own words* to translate a piece of writing for the reader

So, each skill requires that different criteria are met.

❖ When quoting, you must copy the source's words exactly. To show that you have done this, you put quotation marks at the beginning and ending of the quote. You may also be required to supply the source from which you have taken the quote.

❖ When paraphrasing, you put the text in your own words. You take each part of the text and translate it in a way that you think will make it more understandable to the reader.

Directions: Read the following story. Use it to complete the activity on the following page.

> *In 1587, the Roanoke Colony was founded on Roanoke Island in what is now present-day North Carolina. It was created to establish a permanent English settlement in the Virginia Colony. Funded by Sir Walter Raleigh, the Roanoke Colony was begun with the help of 110 men, women, and children. It was at the Roanoke Colony that the first English-speaking child, Virginia Dare, was born in the New World. Soon after the settler's arrival, however, Captain John White was forced to return to England to get food supplies. Travel was difficult, and it took him nearly three years to return to Roanoke. By the time he returned, the entire colony was deserted. To this day, what became of the settlers remains a mystery.*

Comparing Skills:
Quoting vs. Paraphrasing *(cont.)*

Directions: Use the paragraph about Roanoke Colony to answer the following questions.

Remember:

❖ When quoting, you must use quotation marks to set off the words that you have taken from the source. The quoted words must be exactly as they appear in the quoted source.

❖ When paraphrasing, you should use your own words to rewrite the sentence. You can change the structure of the sentence, and you can use different wording. Your main objective is to make the information more understandable for your reader.

1. Find the sentence that tells why the Roanoke Colony was established. Quote the entire sentence on the lines below.

   _____

   _____

   _____

2. Find the sentence that tells who funded Roanoke Colony and how many people started the colony. Paraphrase that sentence here.

   _____

   _____

3. At some point, Captain John White was forced to leave the colony. Provide the four-word quote that tells why he was forced to return to England.

   _____

4. Find the sentence that tells what is known about what happened to the settlers. Paraphrase this sentence here.

   _____

   _____

- -

Fold this section under before making copies for students.

Answers: **1.** "It was created to establish a permanent English settlement in the Virginia Colony."
2. Accept reasonable responses. Students should use their own wording to say that Sir Walter Raleigh paid for the colony, and it was begun by 110 people. **3.** "to get food supplies" **4.** Accept reasonable responses. Students should use their own words to say that the fate of the settlers is a mystery.

Revealing a Theme

Project-Based Writing Connection: Take your final project up a notch by adding an overall theme that represents your work and by displaying it in an interesting way.

A theme can be a concept like "Good vs. Evil," or a theme might be a moral like "Never judge a book by its cover." By weaving a strong theme throughout your project, you can really add an extra dimension to it. Think of the theme as the icing on your project's cake, the gravy on its meatloaf.

Perhaps you've planned from the beginning to incorporate a specific theme into your project. If so, you've made sure to sprinkle it throughout all of your pieces. However, there might be another way to go about things. You might be able to look closely at your various pieces and . . . surprise, the theme was there all along! Finding the theme can be a bit like a scavenger hunt.

Once you do settle on your theme, find a way to insert it all over the place. It should be a repeating message throughout your project, a treasure hunt for your audience to find in each piece of your writing.

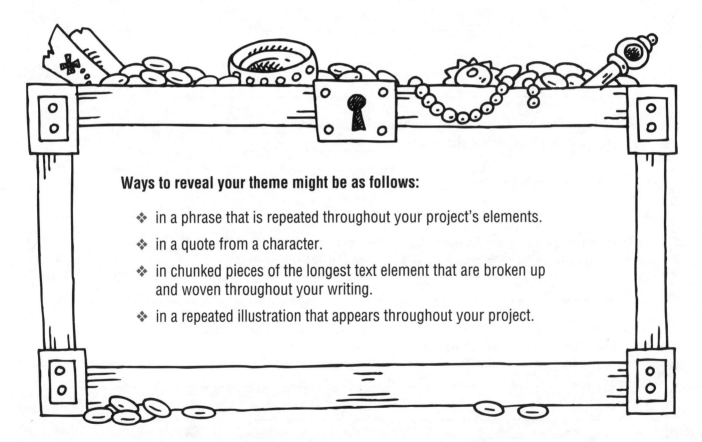

Ways to reveal your theme might be as follows:

❖ in a phrase that is repeated throughout your project's elements.

❖ in a quote from a character.

❖ in chunked pieces of the longest text element that are broken up and woven throughout your writing.

❖ in a repeated illustration that appears throughout your project.

Repeating a theme in your pieces helps your reader see the thought that went into your writing. In order to see how revealing a theme might work, complete the activity on the following page.

Revealing a Theme *(cont.)*

Directions: First, look at this list of possible themes:

> **1.** The Will to Survive

> **3.** The Circle of Life

> **2.** The Power of Words

> **4.** Anyone Can Make a Difference

Now, look at the three excerpts from a student's multi-genre project below:

Story

Ben's Surprising Summer

Ben started his summer not giving a second thought to the owls in the woods, but by September, he had rescued the nest and saved the trees from being cut down.

Essay

Dwindling Resources

The grasslands soon evolved from a rich area of wildlife to an area with no plants, no animals, and no resources. The question then became, "How could the lands be transformed back into what they once were?"

Comic Strip

VACANCY: SPACE AVAILABLE

From the four themes above, which one do you think best describes the samples when examined together? Write your response on the line below.

_____

"Finding" a Poem

Project-Based Writing Connection: By focusing on a key line or phrase that recurs throughout your project, you can create a found poem that will tie the elements together.

A found poem combines your original poetry with a repeating line that is not very poem-like. To create a found poem, you first have to "find" a phrase that you believe really rings true to the heart of your project's topic or theme. You can find lines like that in many unusual places. Here are just a few spots to look:

❖ directions	❖ references	❖ catalogues
❖ recipes	❖ ads	❖ textbooks
❖ horoscopes	❖ letters	❖ cartoons
❖ fortune cookies	❖ e-mails	❖ cereal boxes

For example, let's say you are studying American history and are writing a poem that describes some aspect of the American Revolution. In your search for inspiration, you go into your pantry at home and look at a box of breakfast cereal. The phrase "A Great Way to Wake Up in the Morning" catches your eye. What would a poem based on that phrase look like? How could you tie in that phrase with your historical topic? That's the challenge of creating a found poem.

Directions: Follow each step below to create a found poem.

Step 1: Begin by choosing one of these topics:

❖ parents	❖ video games	❖ cell phones
❖ chores	❖ allergies	❖ homework

Step 2: You will next need to find a phrase to repeat throughout your poem. Look anywhere in the classroom for your inspiration. Look at the posters on the walls, flip through your textbook, or search through the classroom library. All it takes is one phrase to catch your eye and capture your imagination. Write your phrase here:

Step 3: On a separate piece of paper, write a poem with at least four stanzas. Stay focused on your topic, but also remember to pepper your phrase throughout your poem. By combining these two elements — your topic and your phrase — you can create an interesting and unique final product.

Creating Literary Hybrids

Project-Based Writing Connection: By understanding the different literary genres, you can select one that will be most effective in helping you get your project's message across.

Just like Dr. Frankenstein's creation was the sum of different parts, a literary hybrid takes two or more literary genres and stitches them together to create a great story. But before you can combine genres to create a hybrid, you need to think about the distinct elements that make up each genre.

Directions: Identify the main elements of the genres listed below. Think about everything from setting and format to tone and plot. Include an example of each genre. The first one has been done for you.

1. Mythology	2. Young Adult
❖ gods/goddesses ❖ explanation of natural occurrences ❖ created by ancient cultures ❖ emotions can be represented by people ❖ heroes **Example:** elements in *The Lightning Thief*	 **Example:**
3. Mystery **Example:**	**4. Memoir** **Example:**
5. Science Fiction **Example:**	**6. Biography** **Example:**

Now that you've analyzed these genres, think about how you respond to them. Which ones do you most like to read or write? Choose two, and circle them. On a separate page, write a narrative that smooshes together the elements of your two chosen genres. Have fun creating a whole new literary species!

Teacher Note: Another way to do this would be to roll a single die twice. The genres are numbered above. Use the results of your rolls to identify the two genres students must use to create a hybrid.

Mastering the Art of the Article

> **Project-Based Writing Connection:** Use an article as a way to introduce facts about your topic without the presence of bias or opinion.

An article written for a newspaper or an online source can be the perfect multi-genre project in itself because articles often combine writing, photographs, graphs, interviews, etc., in order to give readers a complete picture of an event or person. But before you can incorporate all of those elements into a final product, you need know how to write the actual article first.

Typically, an article is made up of five components:

1. **Headline** — This is the title of your article. It quickly grabs the reader's attention and tells him or her what the article is about.

2. **Byline** — This names the author of the article.

3. **Lead Section** — These intro paragraphs tell the reader the most important beats of the story. The first paragraph contains a hook to grab the reader's attention, and the section continues with the "Five Ws and One H" (Who, What, When, Where, Why, and How) about the subject.

4. **Expansion** — These are the next few paragraphs that build on the first paragraph. This is where the reader can learn about what people have said about the topic. Perhaps there are details like quotes or data to back up the topic of the article.

5. **Related Information** — This includes additional information that might prove interesting to the reader but that isn't important to understanding the initial purpose of the article.

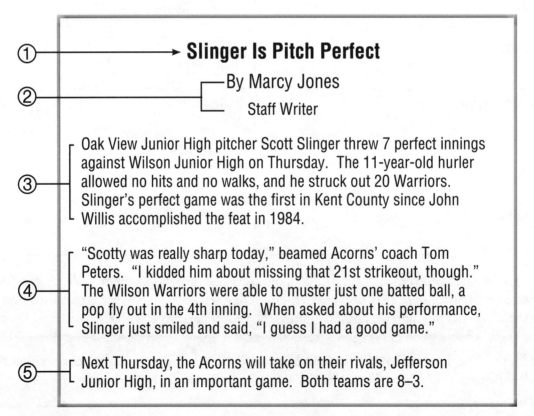

Mastering the Art of the Article *(cont.)*

Directions: Go online and find a news article on an appropriate webpage. A good place to look would be *http://www.cnn.com/studentnews/*. Click on an article that you may be interested in. Cut and paste it into a word-processing document. Then do the following:

1. Use the features in your word-processing program to highlight certain elements of the article according to the color code below:

   | **Who** | – blue | | **Where** | – yellow |

   | **What** | – green | | **Why** | – orange |

   | **When** | – red | | **How** | – pink |

2. Then, underline the hook.

3. Next, read through the article again and **boldface** any quotes or other evidence that serves as details for the topic.

Directions: Once you have researched the topic you have chosen for your advocacy project, write an outline for a newspaper article on your topic. Include the headline and also the type of information you will include in the lead section and in the expansion section.

Rules to Remember

When thinking about your news article, remember these three rules of thumb for journalism:

1. **No bias.**

   Stick to the facts; don't include your opinion for one side or the other. As a writer, pretend that you are the news anchor, just reporting the facts.

2. **Pick an angle and stick to it.**

   Decide the article's point of view and don't drift from it.

3. **Keep it simple and unemotional.**

   Many writing elements — like metaphors, similes, emotion, visualization, concrete description, or personal experience — are not suited to a news article.

Conducting a Movement Survey

Project-Based Writing Connection: This activity will help you do research by gauging public opinion about a topic.

In this activity, your class will vote on issues with their bodies by moving to different areas in the classroom. This offers you a quick, visual way of "taking the temperature of the class" on important issues. After conducting the survey, hold a class discussion about the results. This will allow your classmates to explain their choices.

Tip: Conduct the survey twice: once *before* your classmates learn more about the topic (in order to gauge prior knowledge), and once *after* you have presented evidence about the topic (in order to see if their opinions have changed).

For example, imagine that the topic is "dress codes in school." Let's say you are already researching the pros and cons of a school dress code, but you would like to know the opinion of the class before you present any evidence to them.

Here is some language that you can use to conduct a movement survey:

Before you all came into the classroom, I put up two signs: one says "Pro," and the other says "Con." You can see them on either side of the room.

The topic I'm going to be discussing is whether or not schools should have a dress code.

When I give you the signal, you can vote by standing under the sign that matches your opinion.

❖ If you believe that there is reason why schools should have a dress code, please quietly go stand under the "Pro" sign.

❖ If you believe, without a doubt, that schools should not have a dress code, then go stand under the "Con" sign.

❖ If you are undecided, please go stand in the middle of the two groups in the back of the room.

Directions: Use the form on page 32 to conduct a movement survey in your classroom. Reference the cheat sheet provided on page 31 in order to lead a respectful, informative classroom discussion about the results of the survey.

Conducting a Movement Survey *(cont.)*

After conducting the movement survey, you can then lead the class in a discussion about the results. When you permit the participants in the survey to give their rationale for choosing the sides they did, this will provide you with further evidence for your research project. Take notes on what people say, and write down direct quotes whenever possible.

When conducting the discussion part of your survey, it's important to allow one side to talk and the other side to respond *to that point alone*. This is called "refutation," and it is a vital part of a persuasive counterargument. A back-and-forth exchange of dialogue on a key point might look like this:

Student A: The dress code is important because it puts us all on an even level of appearance.

Student B: That's an interesting point, and I agree that it evens things out, but it doesn't allow for individuality and diversity in appearance.

Use this cheat sheet to keep the discussion respectful and on track:

Here are some guidelines your classmates should keep in mind:
❖ You are agreeing and disagreeing with points, not with people.
❖ If you disagree with a point, that doesn't mean the point isn't important.
❖ People are more likely to listen if you are diplomatic and respectful.

Here are some sentence stems for discussion:

To disagree:
❖ I realize not everyone will agree with me, but . . .
❖ That's an interesting idea, but maybe . . .
❖ I see it a little differently because . . .

To agree:
❖ I agree with what _____ said about . . .
❖ I was wondering/thinking about that, too.
❖ Can I just take that point a step further and say that . . .

To encourage participation:
❖ We haven't heard from you yet.
❖ Could you give me an example of that?

To add to the thought:
❖ May I add something here?
❖ Maybe you could . . .

To clarify:
❖ Could you repeat/rephrase that?
❖ In other words, you think that . . .

Conducting a Movement Survey *(cont.)*

A movement survey is a way for you to conduct a poll by asking people to stand in a place that represents their opinion on a topic.

Step 1:

On the day *before* the activity, write down a little information to read to your pollsters to give them the context of your topic:

❖ Write one sentence that argues **FOR** a side: _____

_____

❖ Write one sentence that argues **AGAINST** that side: _____

_____

❖ Write a question you want to ask your pollsters: _____

_____

Step 2:

On the day of the activity, hang a sign in the room on one wall marked "PRO." Put a sign marked "**CON**" on the opposite wall. You can decorate your sign with symbols or drawings related to your topic.

Step 3:

Read your information to your pollsters to give them background information on your topic.

Step 4:

Ask students to go stand under the sign that best represents their opinion.

Step 5:

Ask people to give other reasons why they believe the way they do. If you write down the best argument you hear word-for-word, you can use the quote as evidence in your essay.

Number of students who stood under the **PRO** sign: _____

❖ The best argument from the **PRO** side: _____

_____

Number of students who stood under the **CON** sign: _____

❖ The best argument from the **CON** side: _____

_____

Use the information above as evidence for your research, advocacy, or persuasive essays.

Learning from the Experts

Project-Based Writing Connection: Use all of the resources available, you to explore an issue or subject. These days, that can mean watching videos of experts from all over the world as they offer their takes on your topic.

What if there were a website that gave you access to the greatest experts of our time? What if you could watch videos and learn from these experts on every field imaginable? Well, that's what *ted.com* is: an amazing collection of videos that have been recorded at TED conferences all across the country.

"TED" stands for "Technology, Entertainment, and Design." On this website, you can find recorded videos on all kinds of topics, from how the brain works to cell biology to wunderkinds. Straight talk from some of the most important and fascinating people of our time is just a click away.

Directions: Go to *http://www.ted.com*, and then answer the questions below. As you get your first glimpse of the site's homepage, you'll immediately notice pictures of speakers on the homepage, as well as buttons on the top and a menu bar along the left-hand side.

1. The pictures of speakers vary in size. What do you think the different sizes represent?

   _____

2. There are many different ways to browse through the videos. Go to the left-hand menu. If you wanted to look at videos other people found the most interesting, name one possible link you could click on.

   _____

3. What are three characteristics you can select from to describe possible videos?

   _____

4. What are the six topics under which you can search?

   _____   _____

   _____   _____

   _____   _____

5. Click on the link that reads "View all tags." A *tag* is a word or phrase that categorizes a piece. For instance, someone may post a video that is tagged as "games," "jaw-dropping," and "science." That is, the video will appear in all three categories. How many videos are tagged as the following?

   Activism _____   Humor _____

   Happiness _____   Heroism _____

For more fun, go to the Search bar at the top of the homepage. Type in "TED under 30." You'll find a list of TED speakers who presented before their 30th birthdays. Sit back and learn from fascinating people who, not so long ago, were sitting in classrooms just as you are now.

Creating a Homepage

Project-Based Writing Connection: You can use the format of a website's homepage to showcase many different projects related to the same topic or theme.

When it comes to websites—the ultimate multi-genre projects—there's no place like the homepage. A good homepage includes a variety of information and formats, and it invites and entices users to visit all of the other content on the site.

A homepage should have many elements, and they should be laid out in a way that is informative and clear to read.

❖ **Banner** — The banner runs along the top of the homepage. It often includes a title, a slogan, and a visual that represents the company/person who runs the website.

❖ **Menu Bar** — Often located in the banner, the menu bar lists the main categories that make up the website. These are links that the user can click on to visit those pages/sections of the site (for example, "Home," "Blog," "About," "Resources").

❖ **Links to Content** — A good homepage features a lot of interesting pictures and story starters. By clicking on links or pictures, users will then be sent to other pages on the site to read or see more of what interests them.

Directions: In the space below, sketch a rough draft of a homepage for a website about your chosen topic. Include a banner and a menu bar. Below the banner, include text, pictures, and links that would entice visitors to want to read and see more of what is on the other pages of your website.

21st-Century Connection: With parents' or teacher's permission, a student can go online and easily create a website using something like *www.wordpress.com* or *www.edublogs.org.*

Using Technology to Present

Project-Based Writing Connection: Use a 21st-century, technology-based method to present your project in a way that adds extra appeal for your audience.

These days, we don't just explain what we know through oral presentations or the traditional book report; we use technology to display and communicate our knowledge.

Think about what you would want to watch or listen to or read, and then go ahead and create that for your work. Listed below are three possible ways you can display what you've learned in a method that reflects the age you live in, the Age of Technology:

❖ **Set Up a Screencast** — Using an iPad app like Educreator or ShowMe, you can display an image and record narration. You can then submit it from your tablet directly to the website. A link will be provided, which you can submit to your teacher for viewing.

Example: Let's say your project involves designing your own country. Open up a screencasting app and draw the map of your country. Include borders, the most important cities, symbols to represent resources, and icons to represent geographical features. Narrate as you draw so that your viewers can hear your description of the country. Mention facts and statistics like population and political system. When you are done, send it to the main site and share the link with your class.

❖ **Produce a Prezi** — A Prezi is a step up from a normal PowerPoint presentation. It uses a concept map rather than slides to go from idea to idea. What's unique about a Prezi is that you can load an image that represents your whole topic and then "zoom in" on the details that show off your knowledge on that topic. If you go to *http://prezi.com*, you can see examples of this cool presentation software. You can create your presentation for free, and it's stored on the web, always there for you and your teacher to access it.

Example: If your project is about saving an endangered species, you can upload an image of the animal and zoom in on specific features. Zoom in on its eye to learn more about how we see the animal in myths and stories. Zoom in to its claw to learn more about how humans endanger its existence. This will give your audience a micro- and macro-understanding of your topic.

❖ **Make a Movie** — There are many ways to create a digital movie. Whether you are using iMovie on a Mac or producing a free, web-based, 30-second movie using Animoto, you have options.

Example: Imagine you have written a letter to a local politician about nutrition in school lunches. Let's say you get the chance to meet him and shake his hand. Record your progress through photographs. Get a picture of yourself sending off the letter, shaking his hand, and cutting a ribbon on a new school cafeteria. Whatever your journey through your project was, find visuals to represent each step. Upload them into Animoto, add some copyright-free music from a site like *www.Soundzabound.com,* and watch a 30-second narrative of your work in pictures and music. Send the link to your teacher.

Directions: Let's say your subject is texting while on the move (walking, riding a bicycle, riding a skateboard, etc.). Think about your position on this activity. Then think about which of the above methods would be the best way to give a presentation on this subject. Give a complete answer on a separate piece of paper.

Writing a Recipe for "Success"

Project-Based Writing Connection: Use the format and elements of recipes to examine a theme or topic in a unique way.

We all know what the average recipe looks like, but have you ever thought of using that format to describe the ingredients of something that you couldn't touch or that wasn't meant to be eaten?

Recipes usually include a few standard elements and often look like this:

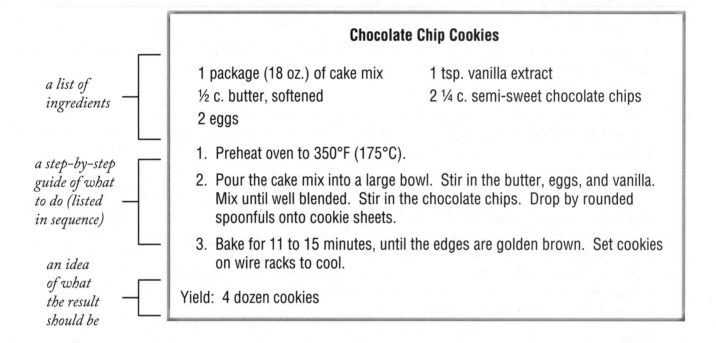

a list of ingredients

a step-by-step guide of what to do (listed in sequence)

an idea of what the result should be

Chocolate Chip Cookies

1 package (18 oz.) of cake mix   1 tsp. vanilla extract
½ c. butter, softened   2 ¼ c. semi-sweet chocolate chips
2 eggs

1. Preheat oven to 350°F (175°C).

2. Pour the cake mix into a large bowl. Stir in the butter, eggs, and vanilla. Mix until well blended. Stir in the chocolate chips. Drop by rounded spoonfuls onto cookie sheets.

3. Bake for 11 to 15 minutes, until the edges are golden brown. Set cookies on wire racks to cool.

Yield: 4 dozen cookies

Now, what if you were to use the traditional recipe format to describe what goes into something more abstract, such as "imagination" or "success"? You would first need to ask yourself the following questions:

❖ What are the ingredients that make up this abstract idea?

❖ How much of each ingredient is required?

❖ How many will the recipe serve?

❖ What are the stove settings and the cooking times?

Directions: Use page 37 to create a recipe for something that can't be eaten or touched.

Writing a Recipe for "Success" *(cont.)*

Directions: It's time to create your own recipe for an intangible thing — that is, something you can't see, touch, taste, or smell.

First, choose one of these invisible, untouchable, untasteable topics. Circle your choice.

Creativity   Hope   Kindness   Intelligence   Friendship   Loyalty   Success

Next, use the template below to create a recipe for your topic. Think about how your chosen topic makes you feel. Don't be afraid to think outside of the box and be creative.

For authenticity, incorporate at least seven of these cooking terms into your recipe:

c. (cup)	stir	pour	sauté
tsp. (teaspoon)	combine	crack	steam
Tbsp. (tablespoon)	whisk	glaze	boil
lb. (pound)	beat	preheat	scald
a pinch	sift	bake	heat
a dash	add	sear	cool

How to Make _____

Ingredients:

To cook:

Yield:

Reading and Writing a Script

Project-Based Writing Connection: You can use the script format to create characters who are affected by, talking about, or in some other way dealing with a topic or theme.

A *script* is a written version of a visually performed medium (a play, a television show, a movie, etc.). In addition to the dialogue (the lines the actors speak), a script also includes the setting (where the action takes place) and stage directions (how the dialogue is spoken, how the actors move through the scene, etc.).

Here is an excerpt from a script of a young-adult movie called *Vampire Middle School*.

(EDMUND stands by the lockers, looking around for the 8th-grader who caught his eye. Suddenly ELLA walks by, and EDMUND immediately puts on a smoldering smile and winks.)

EDMUND

Hey, Ella, going to science class?

ELLA

Um, do you have something in your eye?

EDMUND

(dropping the Romeo routine)

No, I, er… well….

ELLA

Hey, you know, you could use some sun. You should get out more!

(ELLA walks away, the sound of her rejection echoing through the halls of the school.)

So to write a script takes the following elements:

1. the character names (in all caps)

2. the stage directions (in parentheses)

3. the dialogue (not in quotation marks)

Directions: On a separate sheet of paper, continue the scene by having the two characters exchange some new lines of dialogue. Remember to include the three components — character names, stage directions, and dialogue — formatted properly.

Mimicking an Artist's Style

 Project-Based Writing Connection: Use this skill to illustrate a topic or a theme in your project or to provide insight into cultural aspects of a time period.

You can find art by famous artists that mirrors the subject matter, theme, time period, or mood of a project. You can also create art in the style of the artist you choose. This activity will help you learn about some of the amazing artists out there and will teach you a method for studying an artist's style.

You are going to be asked to a mimic one particular artist. Working with a partner, you will need to identify the qualities that are seen in many of that artist's work and copy those into an original piece you will create.

Directions:

1. Find a partner and draw an artist's name out of a hat. On the sheet, you will see a list of three pieces by that artist. Write the name of the artist and the titles of the artwork here:

   _____

   _____

   _____

2. Find out a little bit about this artist and take notes on the back of this paper. When did he or she live? What was his or her painting style called? Did he or she work with things other than paint and canvas? Why did this artist paint the way he or she did?

3. Look at the paintings by this artist online, and if you are able, print them out. In your notes on the back of this page, create a list of at least five characteristics that can be found in some or all of the pieces. Consider elements such as color palette, use of space, subject matter, medium, mood, and style.

4. Copy the most important information from steps 1, 2, and 3 neatly onto a notecard or piece of paper.

> **Examples of Artists**
>
> Salvador Dalí
>
> Vincent van Gogh
>
> Katsushika Hokusai
>
> Roy Lichtenstein
>
> Henri Matisse
>
> Grandma Moses
>
> Georgia O'Keefe
>
> Piet Mondrian
>
> Faith Ringgold
>
> Norman Rockwell
>
> Andy Warhol
>
> Grant Wood
>
> Qui Ying

5. On a blank piece of paper, work with your partner to create a piece of art that is like the artist's work, using the five characteristics as a guide. You can even include things from one or more of the paintings as long as your art is mostly original.

6. The class will set up a gallery where everyone can appreciate and learn about the different qualities in all the studied artists. Name your art and put it up on the wall along with the sheet of information you have prepared.

Another Idea: If you do not wish to create original artwork, you can reproduce a piece of art using a grid as a guide. On a copy of one of the paintings, lay out a grid. Then, on an 8 ½" x 11" sheet of paper, use the squares of the grid as a guide to sketch out one of the paintings into a duplicate. Color in your re-creation of the artist's work.

Using an Illuminated Letter

Project-Based Writing Connection: You can use an illuminated letter to add a visual element to the final draft of a written piece.

An *illuminated letter* is an illustration of a letter, often the first letter of chapter or book. Symbols and icons are drawn into the letter as a way of visually displaying the idea of the text that follows. During the Middle Ages, the illuminated letter became a beautiful art form that allowed people, even those who could not read well, to comprehend the main idea of the material in the books before them.

For instance, let's say that a pamphlet was printed about England's king issuing a new law about taxes on people's harvests. The first letter of the pamphlet might look like the letter shown in the box to the right:

Illuminated letters use symbols to give visual hints to the reader. You can use this idea in your projects. An illuminated letter is a great way to illustrate your main idea in a piece of writing.

Directions: Look at the illuminated letter to the right. If you saw this letter appear in an essay, what do you think the essay would be about? Write your predictions on the lines that follow.

_____

_____

_____

_____

Now, let's practice this concept by creating an illuminated letter based on a topic you know a lot about: yourself. Using the first letter of your first name, create a block letter. Then design and fill the rest of the space with symbols that represent you.

Using an Illuminated Border

Project-Based Writing Connection: To visually tie a project together, add a border around the final draft of your writing or around the container that houses your project.

Much like an illuminated letter, an *illuminated border* can be used to add visual meaning to a written piece. However, by using the margins of a document, an illuminated border frames the text. It creates a decorative picture around the page. This allows the artist to depict not only symbols, but also landscapes or scenes, much in the same way a comic book artist of today will sequence a story.

Remember, the illuminated border always stays focused on the main idea of the text.

Directions: Look at the page below. Inside the page, there is a paragraph about technology. In the framed border surrounding the paragraph, create an illuminated border that captures the main idea of the paragraph.

> *It is important to use technology in schools. Some argue that not every student has access to technology, and that is why we should not use it for everyday classroom work. However, the fact is that students don't have libraries in their homes either, and yet schools still teach students how to read. Similarly, the very fact that some students do not have access makes it all the more important to use technology in schools. Who else is going to teach students how to use technology responsibly? The Internet, computers, even cell phones should all have a purpose in school, because they all have a purpose in the world outside of school. If we want school to really prepare us for the "real world," school needs to incorporate the tools that we already use beyond its walls.*

Creating a Comic Strip

Project-Based Writing Connection: Through illustrations and brief text, a comic strip or a page from a graphic novel can highlight the most important points of the narrative.

You can take inspiration from the look of comic books and graphic novels in order to add a fresh visual element to a text-heavy project. These formats perfectly combine visual elements with writing, and they offer a great way to illustrate the main idea (or the most suspenseful part) of a narrative.

The comic strip below is an example of a way to illustrate a key moment in the poem "The Midnight Ride of Paul Revere."

By illustrating these moments from this poem in frames, the artist is showing what he or she believes to be the most important part of the poem. This guides the reader/viewer to a more complete understanding of the poem.

He springs to the saddle, the bridle he turns,
But lingers and gazes, till full on his sight
A second lamp in the belfry burns!

Teacher Note: Distribute copies of the comic strip template on page 43 for your students. Have them read and follow the directions on that page.

21st-Century Connection: You may also choose to use an online comic strip program. Try one of the following, which are free:

❖ *http://www.makebeliefscomix.com/Comix/*

❖ *http://www.readwritethink.org/files/resources/interactives/comic/*

❖ *http://www.stripcreator.com/make.php*

There are other comic programs that provide more creative control to the user but may not be free. An example would be such as Comic Life (available through the Apple iLife suite), which allows users to convert photos into comic-book-like illustrations and provides numerous templates featuring varying layouts.

Creating a Comic Strip *(cont.)*

Directions: Use the template below to create frames for a comic strip based on your topic. First, you have to decide what are the most important elements of the story or argument to draw. Then, you have to decide on the visual style of your drawing.

Here is a list of elements to focus on:

Story Elements	Writing Devices	Camera Angles
❖ plot	❖ hook	❖ close-ups
❖ setting	❖ sequence	❖ ¾ shots
❖ characters	❖ suspense	❖ long shots
❖ descriptions	❖ foreshadowing	❖ foreground vs. background
❖ conflict	❖ zooming in on a moment	
❖ resolution	❖ dialogue	
❖ theme		

Making a Flip Book

Project-Based Writing Connection: A flip book can be the perfect way to show — both textually and visually — a sequence of steps or events.

A flip book is a mini project in itself that includes both writing and art in order to describe a sequence of steps or events. These steps can form a how-to description, a summary of a novel, a chronological timeline, or even a scientific guide through a particular process. The different pages of the flip book can also be used to illustrate the different elements of a complex issue.

In order to make a flip book, you need these materials:

- ❖ several sheets of paper
- ❖ stapler
- ❖ drawing supplies
- ❖ pen

Then, follow these steps:

1. Stagger several sheets of paper in order to create visible tabs.

2. Next, fold the sheets to create a booklet of consistently spaced tabs.

3. Staple the booklet's folded edge.

4. On the cover, give your flip book a title (the name of the book, the name of the process being described, etc.). Also write your name.

5. Label the tabs by section or chapter.

6. Fill in your summaries, responses, and art.

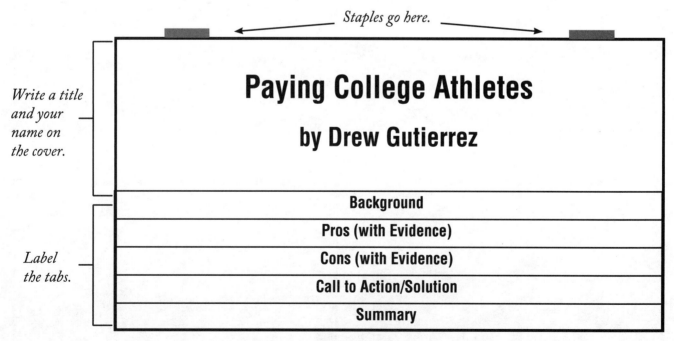

Teacher Note: Students can also go online to create a flip book at the following site:
http://www.readwritethink.org/files/resources/interactives/flipbook/.

Wrapping It All Up

 Project-Based Writing Connection: A container provides an attractive way to present your final project visually, while also tying all of its individual elements together.

Finding a visual way to present your project is important when getting ready to turn in the final results. The package or container in which you house your work is another opportunity to show what you know. It's like the punctuation at the end of the sentence or the glue that holds it all together. It's a visual way to really send home your message with your audience.

Directions: In the activity below, draw lines to match the container with its appropriate topic. The first one has been done for you.

Pizza Box with essays inserted inside	**Pollution**
Clothes Hanger with essays dangling below at different levels	**Body Image**
Globe with a collage of essays taped onto its surface	**Childhood Obesity**
Mailbox with essays, charts, and graphs taped to it	**Ocean Levels**
Trash Can Lid with essays glued to the inside	**Getting Rid of the Post Office**

Now, what containers would you pick for the following topics?

1. Protecting endangered species _____

2. Global warming _____

3. Cell phones in schools _____

4. Library closures _____

Ask Yourself: What container could you use to house your own project? How is that container a symbol of your project, and how does it help your audience connect with your topic?

Cornell Notes

Project-Based Writing Connection: This resource can help you organize and process information for any project.

Cornell notes are a great way to organize your researched information. You use Cornell notes to . . .

❖ **Record key points.** This helps you think of the overall concepts.

❖ **Make detailed notes.** This helps you dig deeper into the key points.

❖ **Write a reflective summary.** This can help embed the information more deeply into your memory.

A page of Cornell notes is divided into three main sections:

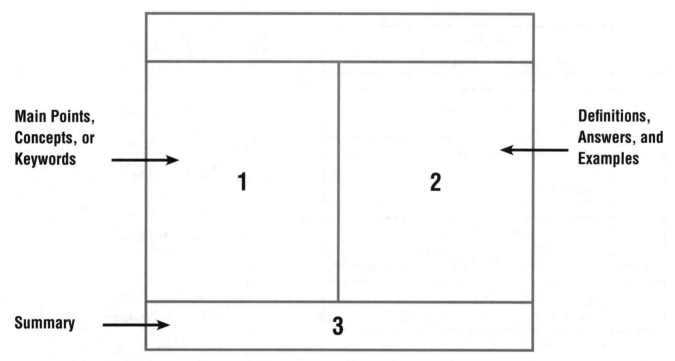

1. **Main Points, Concepts, or Keywords** — This information should be recorded in the left-hand column on the page. Main ideas and key elements (dates, people, etc.) should be included here. You may also use this space to develop questions that need to be answered about the topic.

2. **Definitions, Answers, and Examples** — This information should be recorded in the right-hand column. Use this large space to explain the terms and answer the questions listed on the left. Be brief and clear. Do this by using bullets or short phrases and skipping lines between ideas.

3. **Summary** — A brief summary of the topic and your finding should be recorded here. Aim to summarize the information in three sentences or less.

Reminder: Don't forget to put such information as your name, the date, and your topic along the top of your page of Cornell notes.

You can use these instructions to create your own Cornell notes on a piece of lined paper, or you can use the blank template provided on page 47.

Cornell Notes *(cont.)*

Directions: Use this template to help organize your research about your topic.

Name:	Date:
Topic:	Class:

Main Points, Concepts, or Keywords:	Definitions, Answers, and Examples:

Summary:

Bibliographies

> **Project-Based Writing Connection:** This resource shows you how to cite the different types of information used in research projects. (Blank templates are included on page 49.)

Every research essay needs evidence, and every piece of evidence came from somewhere. It's important, therefore, to learn how to create a proper bibliography. Keep the following resource on hand for your bibliographical reference needs.

Bibliography Cheat Sheet

Book

Author's last name, first name. *Book title.* City of publication: Publishing company, Publication date. Pages. Medium.

Example:

Collins, Suzanne. *The Hunger Games.* New York: Scholastic Press, 2008. 12–23. Print.

Article in a Newspaper or Magazine

Author's last name, first name. "Article title." *Periodical title.* Month, Year: Pages of actual article. Medium.

Example:

Smith, John. "Dancing with the Cars." *Car and Driver Monthly.* April, 2003: 12–14. Print.

Website

"Name of page." *Name of website.* Editor(s) (if available). Date of publication or of the latest update (day/month/year). Medium. Date of access (day/month/year).

Example:

"Book Review: The Hunger Games." *Tweenteacher.* Wolpert-Gawron, Heather. 9 December 2008. Web. 7 March 2012.

Interview

Subject's last name, first name. Personal Interview. Date of interview (day, month, year).

Example:

Spielberg, Steven. Personal Interview. 14 January 2011.

Movie

Title. Name of director. Year of release. Format. Studio, release date of format.

Example:

E.T: The Extraterrestrial. Steven Spielberg. 1982. DVD. Universal Studios, 2005.

21st-Century Connection: The website *www.easybib.com* is a free, automatic bibliography-entry creator. Just type in the information, and it puts it into the correct format. But be prepared: you need to know what information to enter, or your bibliography will be incomplete!

Bibliographies *(cont.)*

Directions: Use these forms to gather the correct information as you do research. You may not be able to fill in every line, depending on the type of resource and the information provided.

Information Source: Book

Author's Name: _____

Title of Book or Selection: _____

Series Title: _____

Editor or Translator's Name: _____

Edition and Volume Number: _____

Publisher: _____

Publication City and Date: _____

Page Numbers: _____

Comments: _____

Information Source: Periodical (magazine, newspaper, etc.)

Author's Name: _____

Title of Article: _____

Title of Periodical: _____

Series and Volume Numbers: _____

Publication Date: _____

Page Numbers: _____

Comments: _____

Information Source: Internet

Author's Name: _____

Title of Article or Page: _____

Name of Website or Company: _____

URL: _____

Publication Date (or Date Last Revised): _____

Access Date: _____

Comments: _____

Outline — Narrative/Story

 Project-Based Writing Connection: This resource can help you flesh out narratives, and it can also help keep you focused on what you need to do to successfully complete a task.

A **narrative/story** is a piece of writing or speech that describes a sequence of events. A narrative can be completely fictional (like a fantasy) or based on truth to some degree. It includes any kind of story — from science fiction to romance to personal memoirs.

Here are some elements to look for when reading and revising narratives:

I. The Opening (Exposition)
- **A.** Hook
- **B.** Characters
  - **1.** Physical Traits
  - **2.** Personality Traits
  - **3.** Inner Conflicts
- **C.** Setting
- **D.** Tone / Mood
- **E.** Main Story Conflict

II. The Body (Rising Action — Climax — Falling Action)
- **A.** Sequential Events (or flashback if using that strategy)
- **B.** Sensory or Emotion Details (sight, smell, touch, taste, hear, feel in your heart)
- **C.** Foreshadowing/Suspense
- **D.** Figurative Language (simile, metaphor, onomatopoeia, personification, etc.)
- **E.** Dialogue
- **F.** Description of Facial Expression, Gestures
- **G.** Transitions
- **H.** Action Verbs

III. The Ending (Resolution)
- **A.** "Tie it all up"
- **B.** Lesson Learned, Theme, Moral, Motto, etc.

Hint! Remember to incorporate these six traits of good writing for added sophistication:

- ❏ Sentence Variety
- ❏ Proper Conventions
- ❏ Great Ideas
- ❏ Voice
- ❏ Word Choice
- ❏ Organization

Outline — Narrative/Story *(cont.)*

Project-Based Writing Connection: This resource provides a visual way to look at story structure. Use it to map out stories.

Directions: Use the story swoop to organize your narrative. Write the most important parts of your story in the appropriate places along the swoop. This will illustrate how your narrative flows from one idea to the next.

The Story Swoop

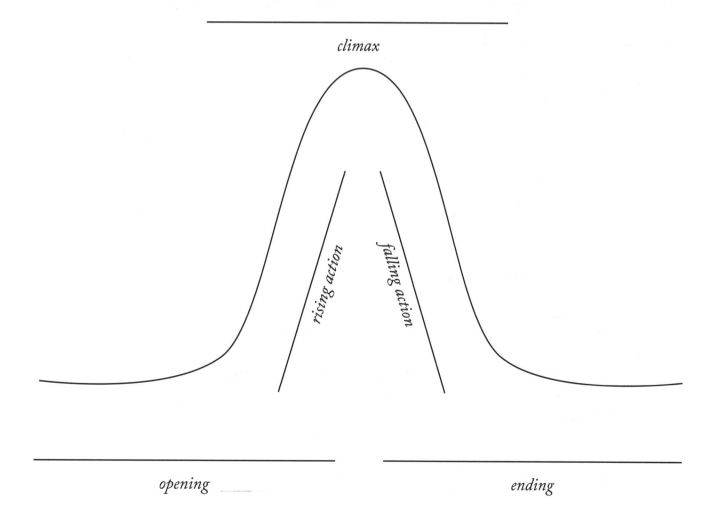

Outline — Persuasive

Project-Based Writing Connection: This resource can help you craft a piece of writing that will effectively persuade your reader to view a topic from your perspective.

The terms *advocacy* and *persuasive* refer to writing that is meant to influence and change minds. Being able to write a successful persuasive essay is an important skill. Use the strongest word choices and evidence in order to increase your chances of convincing your readers.

Here are some elements to look for when reading and revising persuasive writing:

I. Introduction
- **A.** Hook
- **B.** Background information
- **C.** Who is affected by this issue?
- **D.** Thesis Statement (Opinion + Reason #1 + Reason #2)
  For instance: *I strongly believe that the school vending machines should only sell water because it is a healthy alternative to sugary drinks and it is less expensive to buy.*

II. Body paragraph: Reason #1
- **A.** Main Topic Sentence (general statement)
- **B.** Expansion of the Main Topic (gets more specific)
- **C.** Textual Evidence/Proof (quotes, statistics, data, personal experience, etc.)
- **D.** Commentary/Connection to the evidence
- **E.** Transition to next paragraph

III. Body paragraph: Reason #2
- **A.** Main Topic Sentence (general statement)
- **B.** Expansion of the Main Topic (gets more specific)
- **C.** Textual Evidence/Proof (quotes, statistics, data, personal experience, etc.)
- **D.** Commentary/Connection to the evidence
- **E.** Transition to next paragraph

IV. Counterargument
- **A.** Main Topic Sentence (states the opposing side's *best* point)
- **B.** Expansion of the Main Topic (gets more specific)
- **C.** Textual Evidence/Proof (quotes, statistics, data, personal experience, etc.)
- **D.** Commentary/Connection to the evidence
- **E.** Conclusion that *refutes* this point (i.e., why it doesn't convince you)

V. Conclusion
- **A.** Reiterate Thesis (using different words)
- **B.** Solution/Call to Action (what we should do about it)

Outline — Summary

 Project-Based Writing Connection: This resource can help you focus on only the most important parts of a piece of writing.

A *summary* is the gist of a more complex piece of writing. It is meant to educate readers quickly by giving an overview of the most important points. The key is to make it simple so that anyone can understand the issue.

In addition to summarizing the main points of your issue, an executive summary should recommend a solution.

Here are some points to remember when writing a summary:

✔ Don't give your opinion.

✔ Stick to the facts in the original piece.

✔ Use your own words.

✔ Keep language strong and positive.

✔ Select the most important points and disregard points that aren't important.

✔ Consider using subtitles, boldface, or bullets to help organize your summary.

✔ Paragraphs should be short and readable.

✔ The summary should be no longer than two pages in length.

A rough outline could be as follows:

I. Background Information
   A. Purpose of the Report
   B. Scope of the Issue

II. Main Points
   A. Major Findings
   B. Evidence
   C. Methods Currently Used To Solve the Problem
   D. How To Publicize the Issue

III. Recommendations

Outline — Response to Literature

> **Project-Based Writing Connection:** This resource can help you get organized when you write about another piece of writing, such as a novel, story, essay, or poem.

A *response-to-literature essay* is a chance to weigh in on something you have read. There are a few different ways to write a response to literature.

❖ You can come up with a theory about what or how the author was trying to communicate.

❖ You can relate the writing to real life or the time in which it was written.

❖ You can explain your personal response to the writing.

Make sure you know what type of response-to-literature essay your teacher is looking for. No matter what type you write, though, it is important to support your statements with quotations from the literature and explain the quotations.

Here are some things to look for when reading and revising a response to literature.

I. Introduction
  A. Hook
  B. Background information (what you are responding to, who wrote it, what type of text it is)
  C. Thesis statement

II. Body Paragraphs
  A. Reasons supporting your thesis (one per paragraph)
  B. Quotations that illustrate your reasons
  C. Explanations of what each quotation means and how it supports your point
  D. Graceful transitions

III. Conclusion
  A. Thesis statement reiterated and explained
  B. Implications/parting thoughts

The Writing-Genre Matrix

Project-Based Writing Connection: This resource can get you thinking about the structure, purpose, and content of different forms of writing. This helps you choose the best genre(s) for your purpose when writing.

Directions: Study the matrix below, which shows the various elements that go into five different genres of writing: Narrative, Summary, Argument (Persuasive), Response to Literature, and Informational.

Teacher Note: This chart is meant to get students thinking about the overlap in writing genres. The categorization of these elements may be up for debate. For instance, it could be said that "voice" can be found in many genres. Use this resource to spark a classroom discussion about writing.

Genre	Narrative	Summary	Argument	Response	Informational
Hook	√		√	√	
Background Info	√		√	√	√
Thesis Statement			√	√	√
TAG (title/author/genre)		√		√	
Main Topic Sentence		√	√	√	√
Evidence			√	√	√
Commentary			√	√	√
Transition Words	√	√	√	√	√
Voice	√				
Sentence Variety	√	√	√	√	√
Conventions	√	√	√	√	√
Figurative Language	√				
Plot	√				
Rising Action	√				
Exposition	√				
Setting	√				
Characters	√				
Conflict	√		√		
Falling Action	√				
Resolution	√				
Theme	√	√			
Counterargument			√		
Call to Action/Solution			√		

Unit Checklist

 Project-Based Writing Connection: A checklist can help you organize your time and your work so that you never lose sight of your deadlines.

Tips for Using this Checklist

❖ In the "Assigned Element" column, fill in a more general type of element, like "Research" or "Written Piece" or "Visual Element."

❖ Use the "Possibilities" column to brainstorm possible ways you could fulfill those requirements, such as "Survey" for research or "Movie Poster" for visual element. Really try to jot down a lot of ideas in the "Possibilities" column.

Date Due	Date Done	Assigned Element	Possibilities

Using Rubrics

Project-Based Writing Connection: Rubrics can help you understand what is expected of you before you begin each element of a project.

Rubrics are important because they serve two vital purposes:

1. Rubrics tell a student how he or she did.

2. By clearly defining your expectations to students, rubrics serve as preemptive feedback.

Over the next few pages, several rubrics are featured. They fall into two categories:

teacher-created   **student-created**

Both can be used peer-to-peer to evaluate student rough drafts, or they can be used to evaluate a final project itself.

If completed prior to producing the actual project, a student-created rubric can really motivate students by driving home what is necessary to achieve the highest score possible.

Before handing out the student-created rubric worksheet on page 59, distribute copies of the following card to students. It can serve as a step-by-step "How To" guide for students to follow as they create their rubrics.

Creating a Rubric

Creating a rubric for an element of a project (a narrative, an oral presentation, an expository paper, a visual, etc.) is simple. It just takes three basic steps:

Step 1: In the left-hand column, list the qualities that you believe are the most important in order to do well on the project.

Step 2: Across the top, list the rankings that would describe how well a person did. Do this by writing a number and a word. For instance, you could write "4 – Fantastic" in the first box, and you could write "1 – Poor" in the last box.

Step 3: In the boxes of the matrix, write descriptions of what the various scores would look like. Use words that you know.

Using Rubrics *(cont.)*

Teacher-Created Rubrics

Below are different possible rubric templates that can be used with various projects.

Project Rubric

Criteria	Exceeds	Meets	Approaching	Not Evident
Research Quality				
Theme Appears Throughout				
Quality of Writing				
Creativity				
Neatness				
Organization				
Bibliography				
Conventions				
Presentation				

Oral-Presentation Rubric

Criteria	3	2	1
Volume			
Stance			
Eye Contact			
Information Quality			
Intonation			
Speed			

Using Rubrics *(cont.)*

Student-Created Rubrics

Reading a teacher-created rubric is really helpful, but a more powerful way to use rubrics is to create one yourself to evaluate your own project or a peer's project. If you have a hand in designing your own rubric, it helps you to understand more of what to expect!

Directions: Look at this sample rubric. How would you translate it into your own words? What does a "4" mean? What do the words mean to you? In the blank template below, use your own words to re-create a rubric.

Sample	4	3	2	1
Quality of Writing	Sentences are exceedingly coherent. The standards are exceeded.	Sentences are coherent. Standards are met.	Sentences are simple in nature and almost meet the standards.	Sentences are incomplete and in fragments. There are few or no complete sentences.
Ideas and Concepts	There is a high level of critical thinking to the ideas and concepts.	The level of thinking in the ideas and concepts is acceptable.	The ideas and concepts are approaching acceptability. They still indicate a lack of awareness of the content-matter.	The ideas are simple and do not indicate grade-level thinking.

Create Your Own Rubric

Teacher Feedback

 Project-Based Writing Connection: Getting one-on-one conference time with the teacher can help you focus on what you are doing right and what you need to work on.

At times, you might need help with some aspect of your project. Often, a quick conference with your teacher will do just the trick. Be prepared to make the most out of the opportunity to receive such helpful feedback.

Take the form below with you to your conference. Take notes as your teacher talks; this will help you absorb the information more fully. You can use these notes later as a reference when you are revising or finalizing your paper.

Teacher Note: You might not need to fill in every line of this form. Just use it as a guide.

Own Your Own Feedback

Notes on Your Topic/Theme: _____

_____

_____

Notes on Your Thesis Statement: _____

_____

_____

This is great: Keep doing it, don't change a thing! (List skills you've done well.)

_____

_____

This could be better: Reconsider, mull over, overhaul. (List items you still need to work on.)

_____

_____

Based on the work in front of me today, my teacher is giving me a(n) _____.
                                                                        (enter grade)

Think about it: Am I satisfied with that grade?   Yes   No

Due date of final draft, based on our discussion: _____

Signed: _____   **Date:** _____

Unit 1: Teach the Teacher

Teacher Instructions

 The basis of reading comprehension is the ability to read content and then accurately answer questions based on that content. However, an even deeper level is achieved when the reader can communicate that content to another person in a way that person understands. This ability to communicate and instruct is a tool that will be needed for many professions and in many levels of higher education. So why not tap into that skillset now? And let's face it, what middle-schooler doesn't want to be the authority somehow? This unit gives each student the opportunity to be just that.

"Teach the Teacher" is a multi-genre unit that asks each student to select a topic for a course that he or she will teach in a way that engages all of the different learners in the class. While that can be a challenging goal to accomplish (as any teacher will tell you), students will learn a lot in the attempt to achieve it.

This unit is all about the power of student choice. It puts the authority of the lesson in the students' hands, scaffolding each lesson step by step until each student is ready to present an entire lesson and assessment to the whole class.

This unit includes the following components:

- ❖ **"Teachable Topics"** (page 62) — Begin this unit by distributing this worksheet. Use it to guide students in choosing topics that will be both fun and rigorous to research and teach.

- ❖ **"How Learners Learn"** (pages 63–64) — Introduce the concept of how different learners learn. Have students match up the learning categories with various activities, which will help them think about how their topics can be taught in ways that reach different learners.

- ❖ **"Pitch Your Topic"** (page 65) — Have students do research and submit persuasive pitches that explain why their topics are worthy of being taught.

- ❖ **"Create a Lesson Plan"** (pages 66–67) — Show an example of a lesson plan for teaching a topic, and then have students create outlines for their own lesson plans.

- ❖ **"Quiz the Class"** (pages 68–69) — Examine the different types of quiz questions before having students create quizzes based on their teaching topics. (**Note:** Before distributing these pages, locate an appropriate quiz-making website. Sign up for an account, if needed, so that your students can use the website to create quizzes online.)

- ❖ **"Give an Oral Presentation"** (pages 70–72) — Give students tips on the why's and how's of planning a successful oral presentation, which they will then use to present their topics to the class.

- ❖ **"Write a Persuasive Letter"** (page 73) — Direct students to write a business letter to a school administrator. This letter will explain why their topic should be considered as a possible new elective for the following school year.

- ❖ **"Unit Checklist"** (page 74) — Provide students with this valuable resource, which will help them stay focused, on task, and in front of deadlines.

Teachable Topics

At last, the time has come for you to teach the teacher (and all of the other students in your class). Has there ever been a topic that made you think, "Why don't they teach that in school?" Throughout the course of this unit, you will get the chance not only to teach this topic, but also to persuade your teacher and your school administrator that this topic should be taught over and over again — by you, of course.

Now the question remains: What will you choose to teach everyone about? Your topic can be anything from "The History of . . ." (video games, blue jeans, the Internet, etc.) to "How to . . ." (prepare a healthy meal, throw a curveball, master a particular video game, etc.). The possibilities are endless.

Choose a topic with which you are familiar but about which you can learn more through research. After all, the more knowledge and insight you can bring to this topic, the better chance you will have to convince everyone that it is a subject worth teaching.

Directions: Think of three possible topics for you to teach. List the pros and cons of teaching each topic. "Pros" may be how much you know about the topic, how interesting you think it will for others to learn, etc. "Cons" may be that it would be difficult for others to learn, the cost or availability of materials needed to teach the class, etc.

Possible Topic #1 _____

   Pros: _____   Cons: _____

          _____   _____

          _____   _____

Possible Topic #2 _____

   Pros: _____   Cons: _____

          _____   _____

          _____   _____

Possible Topic #3 _____

   Pros: _____   Cons: _____

          _____   _____

          _____   _____

Now look back at your three possible topics. It's time to make your choice. Which will it be?

My Chosen Topic → (_____)

How Learners Learn

Knowing the different ways in which people learn helps a teacher design lessons that are interesting to lots of students. There are seven learning categories to consider, and a teacher needs to be able to recognize them all in order to create effective lessons. Here are brief descriptions of each category.

❖ **Interpersonal:** uses a deep understanding of oneself; is reflective

❖ **Kinesthetic:** uses sports and movement

❖ **Linguistic:** uses language (words, writing)

❖ **Logical:** uses science and math (numbers, charts, and graphs)

❖ **Musical:** uses tone and rhythm

❖ **Natural:** uses a knowledge and appreciation of nature and the world beyond oneself

❖ **Visual:** uses art, design, and shapes

Directions: In the boxes below, create symbols to represent each learning category. For instance, for Linguistic, you might draw a quill pen to represent writing.

Interpersonal **Kinesthetic** **Linguistic**

Logical **Musical** **Natural** **Visual**

Now think about ways you can meet the different styles of learning as you design lessons for your chosen topic. This will make it more likely that all students are interested in the activities that you are teaching. Jot down some of your ideas on the lines below, and then complete the activity on the next page.

_____

_____

_____

_____

_____

How Learners Learn *(cont.)*

Look at the examples of activities below. Match the kind of learning to the activity. Do this by drawing in the box the symbol you created on the previous page. If you think more than one kind of learning applies, draw multiple symbols.

As the teacher, you ask your students to . . .

1. Design a poster to advertise for your topic. **Symbol(s):**	**5.** Write a diary entry from the point of view of an historical figure associated with your topic. **Symbol(s):**
2. Write an original song about a topic. **Symbol(s):**	**6.** Write a journal entry about how your topic may have come to be a part of our world in the first place. **Symbol(s):**
3. Play charades in small groups to act out vocabulary. **Symbol(s):**	**7.** Give a short speech about how the topic can apply to their lives outside of school. **Symbol(s):**
4. Create a timeline of events in the history of your topic. **Symbol(s):**	**8.** Create and perform a dance that illustrates the topic. **Symbol(s):**

- -

Teacher Note: Fold this section under to cover it before making copies.

Possible answers: **1.** visual; **2.** musical; **3.** kinesthetic; **4.** logical; **5.** linguistic; **6.** linguistic, natural; **7.** interpersonal; **8.** musical, kinesthetic

Pitch Your Topic

Regardless of the topic you have chosen, it's always crucial to get it approved by your teacher first. For your next assignment, you will create a well-written, convincing pitch to help your teacher see why your topic is not only an important one to research, but one that, based on your interest-level, would get the highest quality of work out of you.

Directions: Use the following outline to help you brainstorm and plan out the elements of an essay about your topic. Use the results to write your persuasive pitch on a separate piece of paper.

I. **Hook** — Begin your essay with a sentence that will grab your teacher's attention.

    Ideas and Notes: _____

_____

II. **Background Information** — Pretend your teacher knows nothing about this topic. Write one or two sentences to give him or her the gist of the subject you want to research further.

    Ideas and Notes: _____

_____

III. **Thesis Statement** — Try to write one sophisticated statement that says what you want to study and why. Use the following format:

    I want to be permitted to research _____ because _____.

    Give two reasons why this topic is fascinating to you.

    Ideas and Notes: _____

_____

_____

_____

IV. **Counterargument** — Give a one-sentence counterargument that acknowledges why your teacher might be skeptical of allowing you to spend time researching your topic.

    Ideas and Notes: _____

_____

V. **Your Response** — Refute this counterargument. That is, counter the counterargument. Write one sentence that speaks directly to your teacher's concerns and convinces him or her why you should still be permitted to continue with your subject.

    Ideas and Notes: _____

_____

Create a Lesson Plan

In order to engage learners, you need a plan. Many teachers design formal lessons plans for each lesson in order to break down how to best communicate their content to the class. You will now do the same.

The plan you will be creating should include the following elements:

❖ **Objective** — What is the specific skill that you want your class to know? What is the broader lesson that you will be teaching?

❖ **Materials** — List the things you will need to conduct your lesson. This is not only for you, but also for your teacher so he or she can provide you with the items.

❖ **Step-by-Step Lesson** — Give some thought to what you will do first, second, third, etc., as you walk through the lesson.

❖ **Check for Understanding** — Develop some questions to ask students as you progress through your lesson to make sure that they are "with you."

❖ **Assessment** — Create and distribute a quiz to assess how well your students listened, as well as how effectively you presented your material.

Here is a sample lesson plan that follows this outline:

Objective: I want my class to learn how to create California rolls and learn about how Japanese cuisine is influenced by that country's geography.

Materials:

❖ rice
❖ rice vinegar
❖ crab
❖ avocado
❖ cucumber
❖ seaweed

❖ ginger
❖ wasabi
❖ soy sauce
❖ pre-made CA rolls
❖ bamboo rolling pad
❖ knife

❖ table
❖ document camera
❖ LCD projector
❖ map of Japan
❖ Cornell notes

Step-by-Step Lesson: 1. Introduce materials. **2.** Discuss Japanese geography. Ask students to predict what foods are eaten in Japan, based on its location and land. **3.** Lay out bamboo pad and seaweed under the document camera. **4.** Add crab, avocado, and cucumber. **5.** Roll ingredients. **6.** Cut roll into six pieces. **7.** Take out pre-made rolls from a container and distribute one piece to each student. (Mention food allergies.)

Check for Understanding:

1. "What alternative could you suggest instead of using crab?"

2. "Just to review: Why is fish such a large part of the Japanese diet?"

3. "Could someone remind us of the first three steps to make a California roll?"

Assessment: Distribute a 10-question quiz to students.

Create a Lesson Plan *(cont.)*

It is your turn to create a lesson plan that will help you teach your topic to the class.

Directions: Follow the outline below to create a rough draft of your lesson plan.

Objective: _____

_____

Materials:

Step-by-Step Lesson (only fill in as many steps as are needed):

Step 1: _____

Step 2: _____

Step 3: _____

Step 4: _____

Step 5: _____

Step 6: _____

Step 7: _____

Step 8: _____

Step 9: _____

Step 10: _____

Check for Understanding:

1. _____

2. _____

3. _____

Assessment: _____

Quiz the Class

Developing excellent, high-level questions is a great way to assess your own knowledge of a subject. It's also a perfect way to assess if someone understood what you taught or what you produced.

You are going to develop a 10-question quiz on your topic using a variety of different formats of questions. After all, it gets boring for your peers to take a quiz that is delivered in just one format.

Here are three different kinds of questions to include in your quizzes:

❖ A **forced-choice** question is one that "forces" the test-takers to settle on an answer that the test-creator previously determined.

Examples of forced-choice questions: Multiple Choice, True/False, Matching

❖ A **rank-order** question is one that asks an opinion of the test-taker, but it still must be given within a set range.

Examples of rank-order questions: Star Rating ("1 star" for worst, "5 stars" for best), Assigning a Letter Grade ("A" for best, "B" for next best, etc.)

❖ An **open-ended** question is one that gives the authority to the test-taker, allowing him or her to determine the answer.

Examples of open-ended questions: Short Answer, Essay Response

Directions: On a separate piece of paper, create your own quiz based on your lesson presentation. It should be made up of the following types of questions:

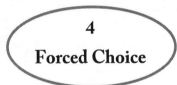

4
Forced Choice

3
Rank Order

3
Open-Ended

When you are creating your own quiz, you should take inspiration from the assessments you've taken as a student. What kinds of question do you believe really challenge you to remember the material? What kinds of question are the most engaging?

21st-Century Connection: Go online to a quiz-making website that your teacher has chosen. There, you can design a quiz using the different methods above. Have your classmates take the test, and the website will score and assess the results.

Quiz the Class *(cont.)*

In the following activity, look at the questions and decide if they are **Forced Choice**, **Rank Order**, or **Open-Ended**. Then, state why you believe the way you do. The first one has been done for you.

Hint: Only answer the "What type of question is it?" and the "Why?" questions.

Question #1. Should students be allowed to have cell phones in classrooms?

❑ Yes, it is their right to have cell phones and use them when appropriate.

❑ No, cell phones are too much of a distraction to learning.

What type of question is it? _____Forced Choice_____ **Why?** I am only given the two choices written by the author; therefore, I'm forced to choose between the two.

Question #2. How should the U.S. deal with illegal immigration? Rank from 1 to 4 ("1" = best).

_____ Create a guest-worker program.

_____ Make illegal immigration a felony.

_____ Build a security fence along the borders.

_____ Make it easier for illegal immigrants to become permanent residents.

What type of question is it? _____ **Why?** _____

_____

Question #3. What can we do when gas prices get too high?

What type of question is it? _____ **Why?** _____

_____

Question #4. Which statement best describes your attitude toward global warming?

A. I don't think it will happen.

B. People and governments should act now to try to prevent or prepare for it.

C. The world may change, but living creatures will adapt.

D. There's nothing we can do about it.

What type of question is it? _____ **Why?** _____

_____

Question #5. What efforts can a school make to help combat childhood obesity?

What type of question is it? _____ **Why?** _____

_____

- -

Teacher Note: Fold this section under to cover it before making copies.

Answers: 2. Rank Order; **3.** Open-Ended; **4.** Forced Choice; **5.** Open-Ended

Give an Oral Presentation

Great speakers don't just wing it and hope for the best. They know where they are going to start and where they are going to end. They also have an idea of how long it will take to get there. To do that, you should have an outline (not a full script) of what you're going to say.

Directions: It is time to present your topic to the class. In minutes, you will need to be able to explain why your topic would make for a valuable school subject that should be taught. Use the next few pages to assist you in completing this task.

❖ On this page, you will find a helpful "Presentation Reminders" card that you can use on the day of your speech to help keep you focused and on track.

❖ On the next page, you will find many tips to help you time your presentation.

❖ On the third page, you will find a template for your presentation.

Begin by writing an outline of your presentation. Base this outline on the lesson plan you have already created. Once you've written your outline, then the real rehearsals begin. When you practice your oral presentation, you need to be aware of multiple elements. Cut out the reminder card below. Use it to help you practice your speech. You can also bring it up to the front of the class with you and put it where you can see it as you present. This will help remind you of what you need to be aware of as you speak in front of an audience.

Presentation Reminders

Volume

Can your audience (your *whole* audience) hear you? Remember to **speak loudly** enough so that the person at the back of the room can hear you.

Emphasis

Are your words flat and monotone, or is there emotion in your voice? How many "um"s, "er"s, or moments of silence are there in your presentation? Are you mumbling? Remember to **speak clearly** and show emotion.

Stance

Are you leaning, fidgeting, or rocking? Remember to **stand up straight**.

Eye Contact

Are you connecting with your audience with your eyes? Or are your eyes trapped to your cue cards and notes? Remember to **look at people** in different parts of the room.

Content

Did you do your research and are you communicating that research? Remember to **stay on topic**.

Timing

Are you speeding? Remember to **speak at a natural pace**, as if you're telling a story.

Give an Oral Presentation *(cont.)*

The issue of timing is an important one when you are speaking in front of an audience. It takes rehearsing your oral presentation over and over — in front of a mirror, for your family, maybe for your friends.

If you were to write an entire speech out on an 8½" x 11" piece of paper, the general rule of thumb is as follows:

> *1 minute of speech = about ¾ of a page of handwriting*

So think about it. If you were doing a 3-minute presentation, you would be writing about a 4-page monologue. (If 3 = ¾ times *x*, then *x* = 4.) The challenge, however, is to actually become so familiar with your speech that you don't need to memorize a totally written essay. Instead, write an outline, and see if you can hit the beats again and again so that your presentation times out right every time you practice.

Directions: Below is an activity that will aid you in timing out your presentation perfectly. Follow the steps provided.

Step 1

Create an outline of your content. Base this outline on your lesson plan.

Step 2

Grab a timer.

Step 3

Stand up and use this worksheet as a cheat sheet as you time your presentation one section at a time.

Step 4

Slow down! Don't be nervous, and be sure to stay in control of your speed rather than the speed being in control of you. It might feel weird, but do it in slow motion once all the way through. Then try it again at a normal pace. This will help you avoid going too fast.

Step 5

With each attempt, write down your time next to the section to indicate your speed and pacing. Get it consistent, and you're ready to go.

Step 6

Repeat. Do it over and over until you don't need the timer to tell you how long you are spending on each section.

Give an Oral Presentation *(cont.)*

Directions: Below is one possible oral presentation broken down into sections. Chunk your presentation into sections, and time each section, using the template below.

Hook

    1st time through: _____   3rd time through: _____

    2nd time through: _____   4th time through: _____

Did you slow down with each rehearsal? Circle your response.   **YES**   **NO**

Background Information

    1st time through: _____   3rd time through: _____

    2nd time through: _____   4th time through: _____

Did you slow down with each rehearsal? Circle your response.   **YES**   **NO**

Main Content

    1st time through: _____   3rd time through: _____

    2nd time through: _____   4th time through: _____

Did you slow down with each rehearsal? Circle your response.   **YES**   **NO**

Questions & Answers (practice with someone asking you questions and you responding)

    1st time through: _____   3rd time through: _____

    2nd time through: _____   4th time through: _____

Did you slow down with each rehearsal? Circle your response.   **YES**   **NO**

Administer Quiz (Giving instructions)

    1st time through: _____   3rd time through: _____

    2nd time through: _____   4th time through: _____

Did you slow down with each rehearsal? Circle your response.   **YES**   **NO**

At the end of each full presentation, add your totals together to see how well you're timing it.

    1st time through: _____   3rd time through: _____

    2nd time through: _____   4th time through: _____

Reflection

❖ Which rehearsal was your best time? _____

❖ Why do you think it was this way? _____

Write a Persuasive Letter

One of the most important elements to include in a "Teach the Teacher" unit is a persuasive business letter to a school administrator. Remember, the point of all of your research, writing, and lesson planning has been to develop a mythical elective for the next school year. Now you just have to put all those skills together.

Directions: On a separate piece of paper, write a persuasive letter in the form of a business letter. Do your best to convince an administrator that your topic would make for a worthwhile class. Remember your writing skills, remember your audience, and remember to be persuasive.

Follow the format below:

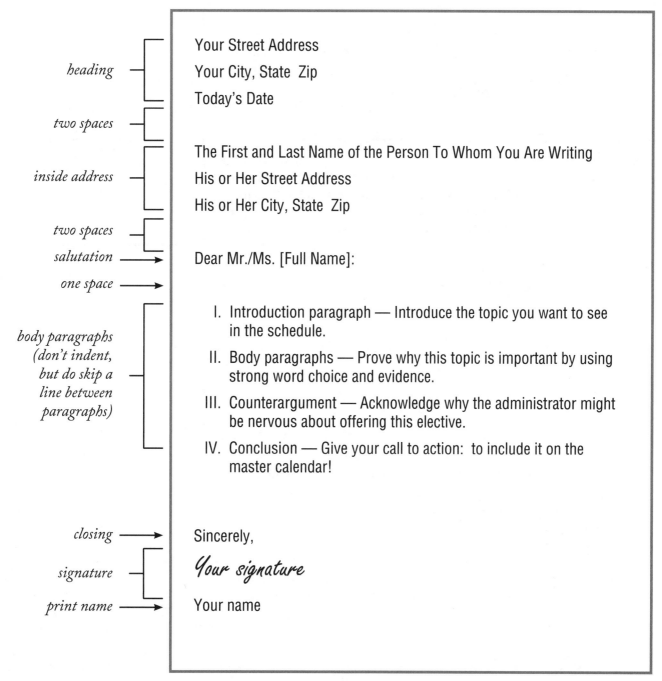

Unit Checklist

Below is a possible checklist for the "Teach the Teacher" unit. It should help to organize your time and work as you move through the process of creating a full project. Look ahead on your checklist and never lose sight of deadlines!

Genre	Description	Due	Turned In
1. Persuasive Writing	Write a persuasive business letter to your teacher pitching your topic.		
2. Lesson Plan	This is a step-by-step description of what you will teach, what you will need, and the activities that you will be doing with the class.		
3. Quiz	A 10-question assessment using various questioning strategies that the class will take and you will grade. (The score will not be counted against the students. You will score their quizzes as an assignment grade that goes toward your final score.)		
4. Bibliography	Include a works-cited page using correct bibliographical format.		
5. Oral Presentation	This will be scored using the oral presentation rubric.		
6. Visual or Kinesthetic Element of Presentation	This can be an activity you are asking the students to do or a visual element used during your lesson plan (poster, PowerPoint, props, etc.).		
7. Your Choice	Choose an additional genre to depict your topic that will be turned in the day of your oral presentation along with the above requirements.		

Unit 2: Career Quest

Teacher Instructions

 This "Career Quest" project is a multi-genre unit that addresses the important concept of career readiness for students. Throughout the course of this unit, students are asked to research possible careers that might interest them in the future and to develop a set of skills that will help them to reach these goals. Students will gain experience with such career-oriented elements as resumes, cover letters, and interview questions.

The purpose of this unit is to introduce students to many kinds of careers, while also encouraging them to explore their own interests. By the end of a "Career Quest" unit, the students will be trained in how to pitch themselves for any position, no matter how wacky or out there the job might be.

Unlike many multi-genre units that require the varied elements to be housed in a container of sorts, the Career Quest unit will ultimately be themed as a job interview. The student is assigned a day at the end of the unit for his or her three-minute "job interview." Through the completion of all its elements, the Career Quest unit represents an authentic process in its real-world connection.

This unit includes the following components:

- ❖ **"Research a Future Career"** (pages 76–77) — Begin the unit by having your students us an online tool that will get them thinking about possible future careers. Students will do research and complete a form that will help them track and analyze the skills and requirements needed to excel in careers of their choosing. (**Note:** You may want to make three copies per student of the form on page 77 so that students can explore multiple career choices.)

- ❖ **"Write a Resume"** (pages 78–79) — Many careers start with a well-crafted resume. Show your students the formatting and information that go into a resume and have them create resumes of their own.

- ❖ **"Develop a Cover Letter"** (pages 80–82) — Here is where students learn about crafting a perfectly persuasive cover letter that can help them secure their dream job. Students begin by assembling notes on who they are, what they've done, and what they're good at. Next, a list of strong, active verbs is provided to get students thinking about writing in a confident voice. Lastly, students will follow instructions to create a well-written, correctly formatted cover letter.

- ❖ **"Answer a Help-Wanted Ad"** (page 83) — Have students write cover letters in response to fictional ads for four job openings. You can distribute page 83, supplying all four ads at once, or you may wish to space out the assignment. You can do this by posting one job ad per day, to which students will apply. You can even make it a contest, with only those students who use proper conventions in their covers letters advancing to the next round.

- ❖ **"The Job Interview"** (pages 84–85) — Give students practice answering the types of question that are often asked during job interviews. Also provided is a list of helpful tips for giving successful interviews.

- ❖ **"Unit Checklist"** (page 86) — Keep students focused, on task, and in front of deadlines.

Research a Future Career

Researching a career is not the same as simply looking for a job. The difference between a job and a career is that a job is something you get to just pay your bills, while a career is a path towards a professional goal. There are often many jobs on a career path. In this unit, you are going to research a career, an area in which you might one day want to become more skilled and invest your time and energy towards doing.

Of course, chances are, you'll jump to different careers in your lifetime as you grow to learn about yourself and as careers change. That's normal. Today, however, you're going to be introduced to an online tool that can help you begin to research a career based on your interests now as a student. It is going to help you figure out what skills it takes to do that job well and what classes you might need to take in high school and college to start down that path. There are no right or wrong answers. It's all about how you want to spend your day and how you might one day want to earn your living.

Step 1

Perhaps the best way to begin exploring the ins and outs of certain careers is to use an online career-research program. There are many such programs available for use, such as those for the Bureau of Labor Statistics (*http://www.bls.gov/oco/*) and O'Net Online (Occupations Online) (*http://www.onetonline.org/find/*). For this exercise, however, we will be using *www/cacareerzone.org*. This website for California Career Zone is a great resource to use, no matter where you live.

Step 2

After accessing *www/cacareerzone.org*, click on the **Assess Yourself** link located on the site's home page. Then explore the following links:

1. **Interest Profiler** — This handy tool asks you what you like to do and uses that information to match your likes with possible occupations.

2. **Work Importance Profiler** — By ranking a series of lists about what you find important, you can discover the type of work environment for which you are best suited.

3. **Quick Assessment** — Choose from six different categories to quickly learn which type of worker you might be. This tool offers an exploration of the jobs that fit your personality.

Step 3

Now go back to the website's homepage and click on the **Get a Reality Check** link. This tool allows you to dig deeper into the financial side of careers. How much money will you need to earn to make ends meet each month? How much can you earn in a particular career? All of this information and more is available to you here.

After exploring this site and all it has to offer, it's time to narrow down your choices to a career that excites you. Once you've done that, fill out the form on page 77.

Research a Future Career *(cont.)*

Directions: Once you have chosen a career to explore in greater detail, fill out the form below. Use this chart to help guide you as you select a career path that will form the basis of your Career Quest project.

Job Title: _____

What knowledge is required to do this job?_____

_____

_____

What tasks would you be responsible for doing if this was your career?

_____

_____

_____

Why does this occupation appeal to you?_____

_____

_____

_____

What do you need to study in college in order to be qualified for this job?_____

_____

_____

_____

What high-school courses could you take to give you an early start in preparing for this career?

_____

_____

_____

Write a Resume

A *resume* is often the first impression an employer has of you as a candidate for a job. It is a one-page snapshot that gives an employer a quick guide to some very important information about you.

- ❖ **Contact Information** — This includes your name, address, phone number, and e-mail address. This information will let an employer know how to reach you to set up an interview.

- ❖ **Objective** — This is a short explanation of your career goals and why you are applying for this position of employment.

- ❖ **Experience** — An employer will want to know if you have had any previous jobs or other work experiences that would make you a good candidate for this job.

- ❖ **Education** — This information shows an employer that you have been studying for this career.

- ❖ **Distinctions** — This section would include any related awards you have won or special skills that you possess. This information should add to your value as a future employee.

One of the most important things to remember about a resume is that is should be clear and understandable at an immediate glance. That is, you should vary your fonts, bolds, and italics so that they make headings clear but don't overwhelm the eye. While there are many different formats you could use, your resume could look something like the following mythical resume:

Joe Job Hunter
12345 Career Quest Ln.
510-555-3445
jjhuntersrus@email.com

Objective: to find a position that utilizes my scientific research abilities, as well as my experience in marine biology

Experience:

October 2010–present

Oceanography Institute of Technology
- Recorded and illustrated species of large sea mammals
- Narwhal expert

April 2009–October 2010

Sea World
- Served as veterinary assistant to all small sea mammals
- Cleaned jellyfish tanks weekly
- Fed otters

Education:
    College: BA University of the Pacific '07
    High School: Atlantic High School '03

Awards: Voted Most Likely to Kiss a Shark • Recipient of the Merman of the Year Award

Skills: Swimming, Diving, Scuba Diving, Drawing, Computer (Word, Excel, PowerPoint), Driving a Submarine

---

Write a Resume *(cont.)*

Directions: Now it's your turn! Use the sample on page 78 as a guide and follow the instructions below to create your own resume.

name ⟶

address ⟶

phone # ⟶

e-mail address ⟶

_____

_____

_____

_____

Objective: _____

_____

Experience:

Write dates in left-hand column; write job titles and descriptions in the right-hand column.

_____

_____

_____

_____

_____

_____

Education:

_____

_____

Awards:

_____

Skills:

_____

_____

Develop a Cover Letter

A *cover letter* is a written introduction to an employer. It is a persuasive business letter that introduces yourself to your potential employer and tries to convince him or her, in one page, that you are worth bringing in to meet.

Developing a great cover letter is all about being able to pitch yourself. In order to apply for a variety of jobs, you have to know who you are as a worker and what your qualifications are.

Directions: In the chart below, use detailed bullet points to give a future employer a snapshot of yourself as a worker. Fill the chart with everything you can think of — subjects in school, chores, part-time jobs, hobbies, etc.

What do you like to do?	
What are you good at?	
What chores or jobs have you been paid to do?	
What regular chores or jobs do you do for which you are not paid?	

After creating these notes about yourself, the next step is to actually pitch yourself for a job that comes your way. Go to page 81 to continue this assignment.

Develop a Cover Letter *(cont.)*

Your cover letter should be strongly worded and convincing. After all, it is a very important persuasive letter that could affect the place you work, the people you meet, the city you live in, and who knows what else! Look at the list of active verbs below and use it as a guide to help your word choice for your Career Quest cover letter.

accomplished	created	investigated	represented
achieved	delegated	measured	researched
acquired	demonstrated	mediated	resolved
advanced	designated	minimized	reviewed
advised	designed	mobilized	revised
aided	developed	modeled	sanctioned
allowed	directed	moderated	satisfied
altered	edited	modified	scheduled
approved	educated	monitored	screened
arranged	encouraged	motivated	scrutinized
ascertained	envisioned	multiplied	secured
assembled	established	negotiated	served
assessed	estimated	operated	set goals
assisted	evaluated	organized	shaped
brainstormed	examined	overhauled	solved
budgeted	explained	performed	sought
built	familiarized	persuaded	spearheaded
calculated	fashioned	planned	streamlined
catalogued	formulated	prepared	strengthened
chaired	generated	prioritized	studied
coached	guided	produced	submitted
collaborated	identified	programmed	suggested
collected	illustrated	purchased	summarized
communicated	implemented	questioned	supervised
compared	improved	realized	synthesized
compiled	improvised	recommended	trained
computed	inferred	recorded	transformed
constructed	informed	recruited	translated
cooperated	inspected	reinforced	updated
coordinated	interpreted	remodeled	upgraded
corresponded	introduced	repaired	validated
counseled	invented	reported	visualized

Develop a Cover Letter *(cont.)*

Imagine that a job opportunity has opened up, and you would like to apply for it. You'll want to create a cover letter that explains why you are the right person for the job (and you'll want to do this without lying or stretching the truth, of course).

Directions: Using the notes you created on page 80, write a cover letter. A cover letter is like a persuasive business letter, so it needs to follow a specific format. Use the instructions in italics to form the perfect cover letter that will sell you as a great candidate for a job.

Your Address

Date

Contact's Name

Contact's Title

Organization Name

Street Address

City, State, Zip

Person's Last Name Only — Dear Mr. or Ms. _____

Paragraph 1 — State the position you are pursuing and how you came to know of the opening. Explain in one or two sentences why the position interests you.

Paragraph 2 — Share the abilities and experiences you have that make you an ideal candidate for this job. Talk about classes, activities, and paid or unpaid positions that relate. Be confident!

Paragraph 3 — State that you are available for an interview and would welcome the opportunity to meet him/her in person. Thank the reader for his or her consideration.

Sincerely,

Your signature

Your name in print

Answer a Help-Wanted Ad

You are now going to be challenged to answer wanted ads for a variety of jobs by writing a persuasive cover letter that is tailor-made for each of them. Some are serious, some are "out there," but your goal is to pitch yourself as if you were absolutely eager to get the job.

Directions: Look at each of the following "Help Wanted" ads. Using the cover letter format (page 82), write a pitch letter to address each one. Use your brainstorm sheet of interests and abilities (page 80) to help encourage you to be truthful in your cover letter.

1.

Wanted
Sports Writer

Do you like slow sports? Well, *Slower Sports Teen Magazine* is looking for a fledgling journalist who is interested in covering the sports beat. From Lawn Bowling to Curling, our readers are interested in the exciting world of slow-moving sports. Interested?

Contact:

Ima Slomover
3425 Sleepy Ave.
Chapel Hill, NC 97650

2.

Wanted
Gaming Expert

From Monopoly to the Wii, we are looking for teenagers who can test out games and review them for our experts. Must have an awareness of what makes a good game. Must be willing to play everything from girl games to boy games, from games rated "E for Everyone" to "T for Teen." Must be prepared to write summaries and rate the games using an approved set of criteria. Interested?

Contact:

D.S. Handhealde
4398 Playstation Place
Los Angeles, CA 97706

3.

Wanted
21st-Century Curriculum Designer

Help! I'm a teacher who is desperate for some 21st-century influence in the classroom, but I don't have time to create my own activities for my classroom. I teach 6th grade language arts and am in need of a person who can develop lessons that are based on the latest and greatest technology. Creative thinking is a must!

Contact:

Mrs. ChalknSlate
#2 Pencil Rd.
St. Louis, MO 95445

4.

Wanted
Superhero Sidekick

Looking for a night job? Looking to enter a life of fighting crime for little or no recognition? Well, do I have the gig for you! Must be computer-literate, quick on your toes, have a gymnastics background, and fit into a brightly colored spandex costume with a cape. Must not be allergic to bats. Interested?

Contact:

Alfred
c/o The Bat Cave
4356 Secret Lair Lane
Mystic, CT 91006

The Job Interview

For any job interview, you need to be ready to answer some questions about yourself. You need to be confident and well prepared. One thing that can make you feel more confident is knowing the types of questions that you might be asked. If you prepare in advance how to address these questions in a thoughtful way, you will be in a great position to make a favorable impression on an employer.

The Career Quest project requires some level of role-playing in its final assessment. Imagine that a much older version of you is being interviewed for a position in which you are greatly interested. To be exact, let's say you are 22 years older than your age now.

Your age now   →   _____

Add 22 years   →   _____

Your age for this interview   →   _____

Okay, now say hello to future you! And get ready to answer some interview questions that will help you get a job that your older self is very excited about.

The questions on page 85 are typical questions you might be asked in any job interview. Remember, that in an actual interview you won't be reading questions and giving written answers, you will be speaking and conversing with another person(s). As a result, you should make your responses sound conversational. That is, use your own voice in your writing. Also, remember to be as detailed and confident as possible.

When you are finished writing your answers to these questions, you should practice saying the answers aloud in a slow and easy fashion. Practice with a friend or in the mirror.

Here are some tips to keep in mind as you practice your interviewing skills:

❖ Don't go too fast or too slow. Use a natural pace when delivering your answers.

❖ Look your interviewer in the eye often. It is important to connect with the interviewer, and establishing eye contact frequently is one way to do this.

❖ Be prepared for nerves during the actual interview. Remember, everyone gets nervous, even those who seem brave. It's just that they do not wear their nerves on their sleeves. Being prepared ahead of time will help you stay calmer, and staying calmer will make you appear more confident.

❖ Thank your interviewer for their time when you're done. Also, be sure to shake his or her hand.

The Job Interview *(cont.)*

Now it is time to give some thoughtful answers to the types of questions you will surely be asked during a job interview.

Directions: Carefully read each of the following questions, and use a short-answer essay form to answer them. Use the hints given next to questions to help focus your answers.

1. **What attracted you to this position?** (Hint: Show them what you know about the job's requirements.)

   _____

   _____

2. **How are you qualified to fill this position?** (Hint: Explain your past experience and how it relates to the job.)

   _____

   _____

3. **How well do you collaborate with others?** (Hint: Think about your past teamwork in school, on teams, helping others, being a leader and also a follower.)

   _____

   _____

4. **What are your strengths?** (Hint: Be honest, but don't brag.)

   _____

   _____

5. **What are your weaknesses?** (Hint: Try to make them sound like strengths.)

   _____

   _____

6. **What can you do for us that someone else can't?** (Hint: Be honest and confident.)

   _____

   _____

7. **Do you have any questions for me?** (Hint: Show them you've thought about this position and what it can do for you, too.)

   _____

   _____

Unit Checklist

Below is a possible checklist for the "Career Quest" unit. It should help to organize your time and work as you move through the process of creating a full project. Look ahead on your checklist and never lose sight of deadlines!

Genre	Description	Due	Turned In
1. Recipe	Create a recipe that describes the ingredients that go into creating the perfect worker for your chosen career.		
2. Research	Fill out research charts based on your online exploration of different professions.		
3. Narrative	Write a short story about a main character who happens to do the job you wish to do.		
4. Resume	Create a final draft of your resume. Base it on your research about the education and experience needed to earn a job in your chosen job field.		
5. Cover Letter	Write a final draft of a cover letter based on a help-wanted ad you've written during the unit.		
6. Oral Presentation	Have a person interview you for a job in your chosen career. Prepare your answers in advance based on a set of questions handed out by your teacher.		
7. Visual	Select a visual genre of your choice and create a piece about your topic.		
8. Your Choice	Choose an additional genre to depict your topic.		

Unit 3: Advocacy Research Project

Teacher Instructions

 Advocacy is a future standard that caters specifically to connecting school life to real life. With the Advocacy Research Project, students choose a topic to study (and advocate for) and also the format in which they want to present their results. These topics can be based on current issues that have an impact on the world around the students, or they can be based on great historical debates from the past. This unit presents both options.

This unit includes the following components:

❖ **"Zeroing In on a Topic"** (pages 88–89) — Have students pick an advocacy topic that interests them. They can choose a current issue or one that sparked debates long ago. With current issues, students will consider the impact their topics have on the world around them. With historical issues, students will step into the shoes of those whose world was affected by these conundrums of the past. (**Note:** You may want to distribute three or more copies of the worksheet on page 88 so students can fill them out for multiple topics.)

❖ **"Write a Thesis Statement** (pages 90–91) — Show how a thesis statement functions in a persuasive essay, and have students create thesis statements for essays about their topics.

❖ **"Conduct an Interview"** (pages 92–93) — Teach students about the importance of interviewing those with knowledge about a subject. Provided are cheat sheets that give tips on how to prepare for and conduct a great interview. An activity page challenges students to read an excerpt from an interview and ask pertinent follow-up questions.

❖ **"Create a Graph"** (pages 94–95) — Discuss the functions of graphs, and examine two prevalent types (the bar graph and the pie chart).

❖ **"Unit Checklist** (page 96) — Provide students with this valuable resource, which will help them stay focused, on task, and in front of deadlines.

Begin by getting your students comfortable with sifting through the news. Pick four students each week to bring in an article, blog post, etc., on topics that are important to them, their community, their country, etc. Collect the articles and keep them organized in a student-created resource library (see page 15). Then, once you are ready to begin the Advocacy Research Project, the students can begin the process of choosing topics by searching through what's already in the classroom.

As they do this, students should ask themselves these questions:

❖ Is there a topic out there that is newsworthy?

❖ Are there at least two sides to the issue?

❖ Can I find ample evidence to back up my opinion?

❖ Can I offer a solution or ask my reader/audience to do something to help the issue?

For historical topics, students can use their textbooks or they can go online to sites like these:

❖ *http://www.animatedatlas.com/timeline.html*

❖ *http://timelines.ws/*

Zeroing In on a Topic

Directions: It's time to choose a topic that is important and interesting to you. Will it be a topic based on a current event that is important in our time? Or will you focus on a historical topic that was debated during its time? For example, should freeing the slaves have been included in the Declaration of Independence? In the time of Renaissance, would you have advocated for funding trips to explore the New World? The possibilities are endless!

Fill out the following worksheet for a subject that you might want to focus on. Don't worry at this point about research; you're just trying to commit to a topic that you can enjoy learning about.

Topic: ⟨ _____ ⟩

List three facts you already know about this topic:

    1. _____

    2. _____

    3. _____

Next, answer the following questions about this topic:

    1. Why is/was this topic important? _____

    _____

    2. Why are you interested in this topic? How do you think you relate to it?

    _____

    _____

    3. Why do you think it's important for your audience to learn about this topic?

    _____

    _____

Finally, think about researching this topic. Where will you go to find your information?

Check off the resource(s) you believe you will use. Don't worry, you're not committed yet. In fact, as you research, you'll find that your list of resources will grow. One will lead you to another.

❑ Books	❑ Websites	❑ Podcasts
❑ Interviews	❑ Videos	

21st-Century Connection: When you use Google to browse information, don't forget the Google Advanced Search. Advanced Search allows you to search magazines, scholarly articles, blogs, newsfeeds, and books. You can search by date released, by keywords, and even by format.

Zeroing In on a Topic *(cont.)*

It's time to finalize your choice for a topic. Write it here:

Now that you have chosen a current or historical topic to research and present to the class, it's time to answer an important question about that topic: How does/did it affect the world? Some topics are very important to one small part of the world but have very little impact on the world as a whole. Other topics affect a whole state or country.

Directions: Look at the graphic below. The various rings represent the scope of those who are/were affected by your topic. Shade or color in each ring to show exactly who is/was affected. You may end up coloring just one ring or all of them.

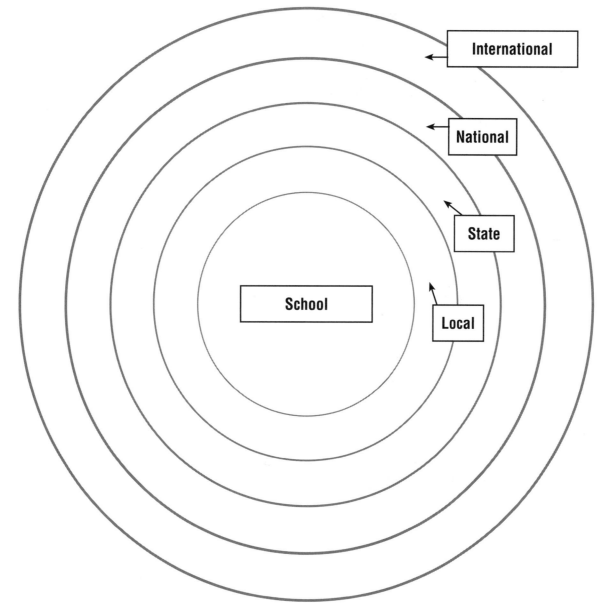

Write a Thesis Statement

For this project, you will be writing an essay that attempts to persuade your readers to see your side of the topic you have chosen. And in this essay, the most important sentence may very well be the thesis statement.

That's because the thesis statement is a map of your entire research essay. It not only tells the reader—in one sentence—what you believe, it also tells your audience the order in which your essay's elements will be found. In that way, it acts like a table of contents for your essay.

A thesis statement is made up of three parts:

your opinion (strongly stated)

your first reason

+   **your second reason**

=   **your thesis statement**

So, if you were to write a paper on why you should be able to chew gum in school, the thesis statement might read as follows:

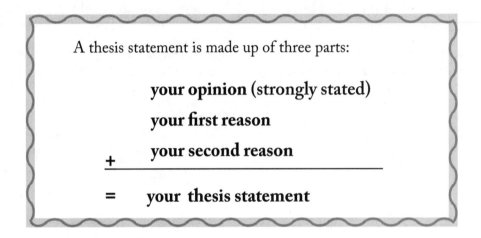

Looking at the sentence above, the reader knows that the first body paragraph of the essay will be on keeping students alert during the day, and the second body paragraph will be on punishing the wrong people because that is the order in which the reasons appear in the thesis statement. See, that is how the thesis statement is like a map or table of contents for your essay.

Write a Thesis Statement *(cont.)*

Directions: Look at the thesis statement below. It is from an essay advocating for the need for school vending machines that contain diverse food options. On the thesis statement, do the following:

- ❑ Underline the phrase that states the author's opinion.
- ❑ Circle the phrase that indicates what the 1st body paragraph will be about.
- ❑ Draw a box around the phrase that indicates what the 2nd body paragraph will be about.

Thesis Statement

Our school should definitely provide vending machines that contain both healthy foods and traditional snack foods, because the lunch lines in the cafeteria are too long, and it is important for students to learn to sort through their options and make wise food choices for themselves.

Directions: Construct a possible thesis statement for a persuasive essay about the topic you have chosen for your Advocacy Research Project.

Your opinion: _____

_____

What 1st paragraph will be about: _____

_____

_____

_____

What 2nd paragraph will be about: _____

_____

_____

_____

Your thesis statement: _____

_____

_____

_____

Conduct an Interview

One of the possible requirements of any research essay is an interview. Conducting *an* interview is easy; conducting a *great* interview is hard. The difference between the two is that the former is a dull Q & A, with you asking set questions and your subject answering with nice, neat responses. The latter—a great interview—is more like a conversation that flows naturally.

For a research project, you can interview an expert on the subject, a witness, an author, an educator, or anyone else who can give you some insight that you wouldn't be able to find out in a book or online. You want the subject to respond in a unique way you wouldn't find anywhere else.

To get a great interview takes planning. There are really two stages to conducting an interview: the preparation and the sit-down. There are tips to help you through both. Use the following cheat sheets to get the most out of your time with your subject.

Interviewing Tips
The Preparation

☞ Research your topic thoroughly.

☞ Research your interview subject and how he or she relates to your topic.

☞ Come prepared with a pen and paper — or better yet, a way to record the subject's voice.

☞ Come to the interview with a list of at least 10 questions. Make sure they are not "yes" or "no" questions.

☞ When you initially contact the person for an interview, don't assume that he or she has the time or the desire to meet you. Be polite and ask if he or she would be so kind as to give you some time.

☞ Arrive dressed for success.

☞ Be on time.

Interviewing Tips
The Actual Interview

☞ Use eye contact.

☞ Shake the interviewee's hand in greeting and when saying goodbye.

☞ Say, "Thank you."

☞ Ask a question that you've prepared, then listen to the response. A good rule of thumb would be to ask a follow-up question based on the response. This proves you are paying attention to the person's response and not just thinking about your next question.

☞ When the interview is over, go somewhere where you can write/type everything that you remember, even if you've recorded the interview. Note the person's clothes, the room, and the walls — everything that can serve to set a scene for those who read your interview.

Conduct an Interview *(cont.)*

In the following activity, you are going to practice asking questions based on an interviewee's answer. Let's pretend that you're interviewing a member of your local Board of Education. Here is a question that you may ask at some point during the interview:

> "What are the checks and balances that are in place when running a school?"

The board member responds:

> "Well, not any one group or person can make the decisions without getting some approval or following a process. This way there can be input from multiple people who care about the issue. So, for instance, if we are deciding to start a new class or something, then we have a lot of different groups that need to help us make that decision and help us see ahead of time what will go into that decision."

Directions: Based on the board member's response, develop three questions you could ask to prove that you were listening to the response.

1. _____

   _____

   _____

   _____

2. _____

   _____

   _____

   _____

3. _____

   _____

   _____

   _____

Create a Graph

A *graph* is a visual display of data.   To create a graph first takes collecting data and then converting that data into the visual interpretation.

For the purposes of your advocacy project, a graph can help you prove your point. You can begin by creating a question to ask of classmates, neighbors, community members, family, etc., and then you can collect the results. (Perhaps, for example, you want to know if people like *Star Wars* over *Star Trek*, or if students think letters are more important than numbers.) A graph can show your findings in a picture that is easily understood at a glance.

There are many frequently used formats for graphing, but the two most common are the bar graph and pie chart.

Bar Graphs

Bar graphs use rectangular bars to show the values of the things they represent. Bar graphs are great for showing the difference between values.

Directions: Look at the data given for a multi-genre project called "Our Love Affair with Fast Food." Use the results to fill in the bars on the graph below. The first bar has been done for you.

Students Polled: 36

Question: "How often do you eat fast food?"

Results:

once a month = 3 students   once a week = 15 students

twice a month = 6 students   more than once a week = 12 students

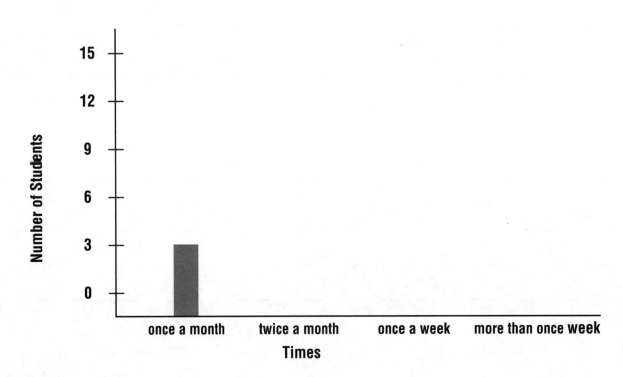

Create a Graph *(cont.)*

Pie Charts

A *pie chart* is a circular chart that is divided into sections based on the values of data. Pie charts are great for displaying the obvious differences when your data values are far apart.

Directions: Look at the data given for a multi-genre project called "Knowing Your Roots." Use the results to label the sections of the pie chart below.

Students Polled: 75

Question: "Have you ever asked your grandparents where they were born?"

Results:

Yes = 25   Don't have grandparents = 9

No = 41

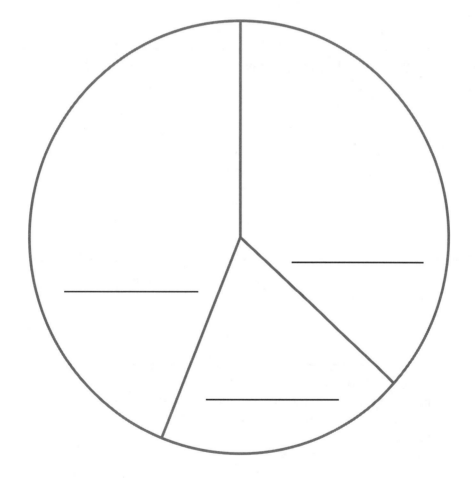

21st-Century Connection: Create your own poll using a website such as *polldaddy.com*. Insert the results into a spreadsheet program (for example, Excel) and create a quick visual 3-D bar graph or pie chart. Cut and paste the results into the typed final draft of a narrative or newspaper article.

Unit Checklist

Below is a possible checklist for the "Advocacy Research" unit. It should help to organize your time and work as you move through the process of creating a full project. Look ahead on your checklist and never lose sight of deadlines!

Genre	Description	Due	Turned In
1. Persuasive Writing	Write a business letter to your teacher in order to pitch the project.		
2. Research	Complete Cornell notes. Include four separate sources, two of which can be Internet-based.		
3. Narrative	Write a short story on the topic.		
4. Bibliography	Include a works-cited page. Use the correct format.		
5. News Article	Write an article about your topic. Include a visual element (photo, graph, etc.).		
6. Interview	Conduct an interview with someone who is knowledgeable about your topic. Include a letter or e-mail thanking this person for his or her contributions.		
7. Your Choice	Choose an additional genre to depict your topic.		